COURAGEOUS TRIUMPH

The Story of
Miriam Gopman's Survival and Success

Fern Ellis

Other publications

The United States Holocaust Memorial Museum, national archives:
Miriam Gopman: The Courage of a Hero and Her Story of Survival

The Los Angeles Times: Educational articles

Simon and Schuster: *English as a Second Language* textbook

The Fugue and *Ovation*: Articles about renowned musicians
interviewed for both publications

The Los Angeles Unified School District: *Public Relations Handbook*,
teacher training video scripts, informational video scripts
for the California legislature

Miami-Dade County Public Schools: Public Relations:
print, radio and TV

Advertising agencies in Los Angeles and Miami: print, radio
and TV publicity

Music Performance CDs:
No Limits: original music, lyrics, vocal and flute
In and Out of Love: vocals of standards from
The Great American Songbook
Jazz in the Lobby Bar, Women in Jazz: vocal tracks on compilation
CDs produced by High Note Records, Taiwan

Soon to be published
The Cosmic Sonata: a novel
Lotus Blossom Zen: an ebook of original sayings

COURAGEOUS TRIUMPH

The Story of
Miriam Gopman's Survival and Success

by

FERN ELLIS

Crazy Bird Music, Inc.

Fern Ellis
P.O. Box 1156
Boone, NC 28607
fernellis@aol.com
www.fernellis.com

This book is based on interviews with the subject of the story over a period of several years, supported by the author's research. It is as factual as the process can make it, based on Miriam's memory.

ISBN-13: 978-1979161282

ISBN-10: 1979161283

Proceeds from the sale of this book benefit
The United States Holocaust Memorial Museum.
Copies have been provided to museums focusing on Jewish history.

Author's Note

I instantly felt an affinity for Miriam Gopman when she walked into a Qigong/Tai Chi class I was teaching in 2005 at her condominium's building. What caused that feeling—the way her generous smile filled the room, the huge presence the petite, vibrant woman generated, or just a simple case of destiny—well, I wouldn't presume to know.

Miriam often stayed after class and would ask how things were going in my personal life. She took a genuine interest in me, but I knew very little about her other than that she spoke with a Russian accent. Her soft, caring manner reminded me of my dear loving grandmother who had hailed from Ukraine, and soon I began looking forward to our Sunday class. By 2007, I felt strongly connected to Miriam. I even began to wonder if perhaps we were biologically related.

During those years I was struggling with my identity as a writer. Aside from writing a few songs, I had abandoned my novel, my journal, my poetry. Quite frankly, I wondered where life's path was leading me. But on my way to teach one day I had an epiphany while waiting in my car at a red light. I looked up, as if to heaven, and made a declaration that I would write again. I said I didn't know what I was going to write about, but I knew a story would come to me.

Not ten minutes later, I opened the door to the exercise room and found Miriam staring out the plate glass window facing the ocean.

"It's such a beautiful day," I said as we both admired the palm trees swaying in the breeze and the crystalline aqua sea. "We have so much to be thankful for."

In her heavily accented English Miriam replied, "I'm thankful every day that I wake up and the Nazis aren't chasing me."

With a little encouragement, Miriam revealed how her family had been captured by the Nazis in the shtetl Tarashcha, Ukraine when she was twelve years old. For the next hour—oddly enough, no other students came to class that day—Miriam recounted her life story. By the time she finished, we were both crying. Now I was certain the universe had delivered the story fate intended me to write. I felt a moral obligation to share it, and Miriam wanted me to write a booklet about her experience to hand out at temples, Hadassah groups and other Jewish organizations.

We met on a regular basis over the next four years for me to interview Miriam. Often she cried. Often I cried. We laughed a lot too. The more I wrote about her life the more I began to see it as a film, so I wrote a screenplay. Although I did not originally intend this work to become a book, I decided to publish it when the United States Holocaust Museum accessioned Miriam's story into the national archives.

After twelve years of working together, Miriam and I have developed a very special bond and sense of kinship. In service to Miriam, I trust her story will become an inspiration to you, the reader, and future generations. Let us honor the courage and triumph of Miriam Gopman, the child star captured by the Nazis who managed to escape from their grip, survive in hiding under an assumed identity, become the sole Jewish survivor of her shtetl, overcome numerous obstacles, testify and incriminate three Nazi officers at the Nazi War Criminal Trials in Dusseldorf that led to their incarceration, and become recognized as an outstanding hotelier dubbed the "Queen of Miami Beach".

Let us never forget!

Fern Ellis, November 2017

Table of Contents

I would like to give special thanks to:

the USC Shoah Foundation Institute for Visual History and Education and to Richard Baum, who helped me attain invaluable information from Germany. Thanks also to Judy Geary for her expertise, patience and kindness in preparing this book for publication.

COURAGEOUS TRIUMPH

The Story of
Miriam Gopman's Survival and Success

A Ukranian scene painted by the author's grandmother who lived near the shtetl where Miriam was born, painted when Miriam was a child.

"Courage is doing what you're afraid to do. There can be no courage unless you're scared."

—Captain Eddie Rickenbacker
World War I Hero,
American flying Ace and Medal of Honor Recipient

CHAPTER 1

Before the War

*E*veryone loved Miriam Shir, a child star of the shtetl Tarashcha in Ukraine. Born to a prominent family in 1929 and nicknamed Musia, the blue-eyed beauty with an infectious smile grew up adored and protected by her three much older brothers. Her parents and grandparents spoiled her as well. Miriam was a free-spirited child who loved to sing and dance, recite poetry, act. The entire community applauded her efforts. Many townspeople, especially her teachers, believed she had a promising acting career ahead of her. And Miriam made it no secret that she dreamed of becoming a famous movie star or a singer. Perhaps she would study in France, like her idol Sarah Bernhardt, the most famous actress known. Or maybe she would find her way to the United States. Somehow, she would make her dream come true. Of that she was certain!

Each summer Miriam looked forward to the arrival of the gypsies, the handsome dark men and the young women with long black hair flaunting colorful skirts and big hoop earrings. They would put on shows for two weeks in the town square where Ukrainian families gathered to enjoy their entertainment and festivities. Sometimes the neighborhood children would also perform. Often the troupes brought singing parakeets and trained dogs that jumped through hoops. Miriam couldn't wait to savor the donuts the gypsies fried in big pots of boiling oil, plus she would try a variety of unusual foods her mother and aunts didn't serve at home.

Invariably, someone would ask Miriam to recite a poem; she'd never be at a loss to deliver a marvelous rendition of her favorite stanzas of iambic pentameter, usually verses from Aleksandr Pushkin's *Eugene Onegin* or the opera *Russlan and Ludmilla*. When the strolling violinists would call her to come on stage to sing and dance their Eastern dances with them, she'd jump right up there and bring the house down. Infused with happiness, Miriam cherished these times.

Before Miriam was born, Lenin had proposed that the Birobidzhan territory in Siberia bordering the northern edge of China should become an autonomous Jewish country with its own Yiddish language, a country Russian Jews would colonize, a place where they could be free from discrimination. But Most Jews didn't want to migrate to an undeveloped location with extreme weather, no industry, no factories and no schools. They preferred not to leave their homes and start all over again working the land to develop it. They didn't believe the propaganda pictures in the newspaper of Jews making gefilte fish, plowing the soil, relaxing. The majority of the Russian Jews who did migrate to Birobidzhan after Stalin declared it a Jewish state in 1928 ended up leaving because the government didn't provide the promised housing and agricultural machinery. The combination of Jews not willing to migrate there and others wanting to emigrate from Birobidzhan did not cast a good image of the Jewish people with other Russians.

Although local Jews were already suffering discrimination during Miriam's childhood—they dared to get together in the synagogue only once a year, on Yom Kippur—Miriam felt no discrimination from her Ukrainian neighbors. The non-Jews of her community didn't single her family out as the only Jews. They told her they respected her and her family because they were different from other

Miriam's parents, Aaron Shir and Rivka Greenfeld Shir, in the 1930s. Because none of the Shirs' photographs were salvaged after the war, this photo may have been given to Miriam by friends of the family.

Jews. These Ukrainians didn't know that Miriam's parents practiced their religion privately, that they prayed in a separate room so their children couldn't observe them. Because a lot of shame was attached to being Jewish, her parents feared that harm might come to Miriam if they taught her about God and her religion. Consequently, they let Miriam celebrate holidays with non-Jews as well as Jews. Miriam didn't think of herself as Jewish, and she certainly didn't look Jewish. Her auburn tresses and dreamy blue eyes set her apart from the dark-haired, dark-eyed Jewish girls and women. She could easily pass for Ukrainian, which would ultimately save her life.

Miriam's father's father, a very wealthy man from the proceeds of his carriage-building business and smithy, owned the biggest private property in Tarashcha: a five-acre plot of land boasting a beautiful two-story house so huge it could accommodate four families. The estate featured a barn with horses and stables, productive farmland inhabited by goats and horses and cows and other animals, manicured gardens, several garages, and a large supermarket-style store. Although there was no running water or toilet, the Shirs washed their dishes in a basin, used the outhouse, and bathed once a week in the *balia* filled with water heated on the stove. For Miriam, lounging in the small wooden bassinette that looked like a barrel cut in half gave her plenty of time to dream about her future as a movie star. Oh, the places she would go and the things she would do.

Miriam loved growing up with her family, her grandparents and her father's three sisters. She admired her parents a great deal. Often she tried to emulate her mother Rivka's fashionable elegance while standing as tall as she could, a reflection of her father Aaron's stature. Her grandfather, a blacksmith by trade, built carriages. He was a wise man with an impressive appearance who believed in the power of education, and he sent all four of his children to university. After the Revolution of 1917, when the Jews were finally allowed to study in Kiev, one of his daughters went on to become a successful surgeon.

As blacksmiths, Miriam's father and grandfather built a reputation making the carriages they housed in the garages next to their market on the premises. The richest people from neighboring towns would travel to the Shirs to place special orders for large carriages. Local residents were always passing by or stopping in for blacksmithing needs. Others came from far and near to buy food at the large market the family women presided over. Mostly Jewish customers, they purchased sweets and candy, chickens and dairy products like cheese and yogurt. While most Jews were tailors or butchers, the Shirs were the only Jews running a food store. But they hired Ukrainians to milk their two cows, sell the pigs they raised, collect eggs from the chickens, garden the fruit trees and potatoes, cook, clean the living quarters and wash clothes. Miriam felt close to many of the Ukrainians. She favored a policeman friend of her father's whom she called Uncle Vladimir and his wife, Aunt Pasha. They were like family.

One day in 1932 officers of the OGPU (the main security agency later renamed the KGB in 1954) banged on the front door of the Shirs' home. Before anyone could answer, several men forced their way in and arrested Miriam's father, grandfather and two aunts. They were taken to jail with other families and squeezed together standing in a jail cell, packed like sardines. The government seized the Shirs' property—along with their animals, the store, gold and more valuables—declared it a government collective farm and made the Shirs labor as farmers on their own property.

But although the OGPU confiscated neighboring houses, they respected Miriam's father and grandfather too much to take their home. They also needed the Shirs' highly specialized blacksmithing skills. Unfortunately, Miriam's grandparents couldn't withstand the shock of this turn of events and soon died at the end of 1932. Aaron was forced to handle all of the business without his father's guidance. He would have to rely on the wisdom passed down to him.

From 1932 to 1934 people were starving, dying in the streets of the Ukrainian Republic and Georgian Republic because there was no food or jobs. Stalin had created The Great Famine (1932-1933), the Holodomor, to force the Ukrainians to give up their land and live on government-controlled collective farms in an attempt to eliminate the Ukrainian independence movement. The Soviet secret police confiscated all food. Those who resisted were sent to Siberia. People even resorted to cannibalism in order to survive. This genocide of the Ukrainian people caused nearly ten million Ukrainians to die. But Stalin accepted no responsibility for the disaster and blamed the counter-revolutionaries. Whereas people had considered Lenin "nice," they likened Stalin to a Mafia king.

Because of the family's prominence, two of the Shir sisters were permitted to run the government store from 1932 to 1937. Also during this period, unbeknownst to the OGPU, which became the GUGB in 1934, Miriam's father managed to secretly work for hire late at night by making gardening tools for Ukrainians in a special oven. In 1937, after Stalin ordered the GUGB to throw millions of Jews, Ukrainians, Georgians, Russian aristocrats, intelligentsia, and high-ranking military officers and their families in jail, the government closed the market. They allowed the Shirs to continue owning the building, but they were forbidden to take on any private work.

When Miriam was ten years old, Stalin signed a pact giving part of Poland to Hitler. That same year, in the summer of 1939, her brother Emile got married. The family walked two-and-a-half miles to the synagogue, accompanied by Ukrainian adults and children, while gypsies played their violins and drums. As far as the Shirs were concerned, anti-semitism posed no threat in their everyday life.

So when Polish Jewish immigrants showed up in Tarashcha spreading news of Hitler's cruelty to the Jews, Miriam's father didn't believe it. He recalled that when the Germans entered Tarashcha during the war in the 1920s, they treated the Jews well. Consequently, he didn't take this war too seriously. But as soon as the radio was introduced in Tarashcha, he began listening regularly. Soon he learned more about the ongoing war in Poland, the pogroms, and he worried about what would happen if the Nazis came to the shtetl. Miriam's three older brothers, the youngest of whom was ten years older than Miriam, were already serving in the Russian military.

Miriam's brothers Simeon (left) and Aleksandr
in their Russian military uniforms

Where would they be sent? How would they know where to find the Shirs if the family had to leave suddenly?

By the time Miriam turned eleven, she was an "A" student. The only Jewish girl in her class, she studied German, Russian, history, mathematics. She loved to read and spent most of her free time in the library because few books were available to be bought. Having learned so much about life and love from her reading, Miriam romanticized about the stage, about men in uniform, about her future as an actress or a singer. She even fantasized meeting the German soldiers and boys that people were saying might come to Russia. She didn't understand what was really going on in the world.

The Stalin government sought to control its people, although it demanded no country should control the USSR. Travel was banned. And Russians were bombarded with the belief that Russia was number one. Influenced by Social Realism, the international art movement that represented the proletarian revolution, propaganda abounded in the form of posters to, as Lenin said, "expose crimes of capitalism and praise socialism."

When Stalin had taken power in 1927—it was rumored he had threatened to kill Lenin after the revolution of 1917—he stressed the importance of education. Soon Russia acclaimed itself the best Soviet Socialist State in the USSR, the smartest country in the world, filled with brilliant chess players, athletes, ballet dancers, musicians, scientists, doctors and teachers.

Like many Russian adults and children, Miriam and her friends fell prey to the government's propaganda. They had no idea the State totally controlled the media and ordered writers to glorify Stalin, portraying him as a kind, fatherly type. Often seen wearing a white suit, he stood out from the crowd. Soon a type of "personality cult" developed, and the masses worshipped the ruthless dictator known as "Uncle Joe." They didn't believe in God. They believed in Stalin. He was their God.

Miriam's passion for performing in musical shows, many of which were patriotic, kept her in the limelight. Singing, dancing, acting, reciting poetry, she became a child star in the shtetl. At a time when it wasn't popular to be Jewish in Russia, Miriam wasn't going to let anything stop her from becoming a movie star. Life in Russia was good.

Then one day everything changed.

CHAPTER 2

The War

On June 22, 1941—a beautiful, sunny day, at around four in the afternoon—hundreds of German bombers bombed Kiev. The noise was deafening. Miriam's family readied the horses and prepared food and water to travel to a railway station an hour-and-a-half away. They packed everything into their covered wagon. But Miriam's mother Rivka, whose oldest son Emile had been killed in the war in Finland, insisted they wait one more day to leave in case a letter might arrive from her sons. Then she would know where to get in touch with them after the family moved. Aaron, certain the Russians wouldn't head to Tarashcha so quickly, agreed. Unfortunately, before the day ended, he learned a small group of German soldiers had marched into Tarashcha. He quickly gathered the family—including Emile's wife Mania and her young child Motyck—and shouted for everyone to grab their coats and hats and run outside into the cellar. Aaron followed after them. They scurried past the loaded wagon to the cellar, threw open the door and ran down the eight stairs. Aaron, the last one in, closed the door. They stayed there for three days, without food or water. Mania's baby, hungry and thirsty, would cry periodically. Mania was so worried the Germans would hear him that she decided to keep him hydrated with her urine. She would pee into a cup and spoon feed the urine to him. The boy didn't cry, but Miriam did, very softly. Her whole body was shivering from the shock of the horrifying experience. On the third day, just as Mania gave Motyck the last spoonful of liquid, soldiers from a special action detachment of the Einsatzgruppe mobile killing unit tore open the cellar door.

"*Juden, Juden, Juden,*" shouted the Einsatzkommando 5 soldiers. "Come out from the cellars."

Scared to death, shaking, and crying and screaming, the Shirs climbed up the cellar stairs. Once outside they came face to face with armed German Nazi soldiers pointing rifles at them. This couldn't be happening, Miriam thought. Why weren't her father's policemen friends coming to help him? The Shirs had always been patriotic, so why weren't the Russians coming to their aid? When Napoleon had invaded Russia, the townspeople had run out of their homes into the snow to help the army chase him out of Russia. But the townspeople felt different now. The Ukrainians believed the Germans were going to liberate them from Communism and the Russian government and create an independent Ukrainian state. They didn't want to jeopardize that possibility by going against the Germans to save the Jews. It didn't take long for them to realize the Nazis had no intention of granting them independence.

Fortunately, Miriam's father spoke a little German and explained to the soldiers that he was a high specialist blacksmith and could help them. They needed his blacksmith skills for their horses, so they let the Shirs return to their house. But on the same day the Shirs escaped annihilation, German soldiers gunned down many Jewish men in different parts of Tarashcha, either in cellars or on the streets. They herded Miriam's sister-in-law's father, a rabbi, along with other religious men, into a synagogue and set it on fire. The men were burned alive.

For several days Miriam watched the Nazis take her father away to work every morning. She and the other women in her family stayed in the house all day. While the women cooked or cleaned or sewed, Miriam read her poetry, recited it, or wrote about her fantasies. Somehow the days passed as they eagerly waited for Aaron to return home at night with food, bread and water he received as payment. At least they were eating well. It seemed the Shirs had been spared. But within a week, the Nazis told Miriam's family they would have to leave their home.

Miriam had a million questions. Where would they go? How would they get there? Would the soldiers take them? Would she like it wherever it was they were going?

The news about the Shirs being evicted spread fast. Because the Ukrainian community loved the Shirs so much, especially the farmers who had worked for Miriam's father, they signed approximately two hundred petitions requesting the family be permitted to stay. This bought the Shirs some time with the authorities, but Aaron realized the gravity of their situation. Just how long they would be spared, he had no way of knowing, and he decided to bury Rivka's most valuable jewelry outside near the cellar. Other furnishings he gave to Vladimir and Pasha for safekeeping. He'd be damned if he'd let the Nazis steal his family's legacy.

For about a month the Shirs continued their routine. No one talked about what was happening, mostly because they didn't want to scare Miriam any more than she was already frightened. Aaron brought home so much food, he could even share some with Ukrainian neighbors who came to visit at night. Miriam was having fun staying home, but she missed the library. She kept asking when she could return to school. Aaron and Rivka didn't want Miriam to know how bad things were, and they always promised her she'd be performing again before she knew it.

On the surface, everything appeared to be going smoothly, although Aaron anticipated that change could occur at any time. And it did. When the Germans occupied Tarashcha in July, one morning Aaron and Rivka were awakened by loud, constant knocking at the door. Aaron, presuming he had to go to work early, got dressed and opened the door. Standing in front of him in a gray uniform with a swastika on his sleeve and SS insignia, a Nazi soldier handed him a piece of paper. Aaron read it and swallowed hard. The Shirs were being ordered to vacate the premises the next day under military guard. Each one of them would be permitted to take a small sack of clothes and some food.

Prisoners in their house that night, family members helped one another pack their rucksacks with only a few belongings. They discussed rumors they had heard about a thousand Jews having been taken to a ghetto. Miriam expressed fear that if those Jews were going to be killed, maybe the Shirs were going to be killed too. Miriam's mother cajoled Miriam, blaming her fear on her vivid imagination and her love for drama. Rivka reassured her that the Germans wanted the Shirs' land and intended to relocate them, perhaps in Birobidzhan. She also reminded Miriam how important her father was to the Nazis, so they surely weren't going to kill him.

When the Nazis and Ukrainian police returned the next day, Ukrainians from the vicinity started streaming into the Shirs' home. The Nazis forced the family to watch neighbors rummage through what was left of their belongings, take their furniture, tablecloths, candle sticks, anything they wanted. Even the Ukrainian police carried furniture out of the home. After the last item had been removed, a tall, debonair, Nazi colonel in his thirties arrived in a six-seat Wanderer limousine. For some reason, he took a liking to Miriam and smiled as he walked by her. She smiled back at him. But when he ordered the family to gather their rucksacks and bags of food, Miriam cried. The whole family wept.

The colonel and his driver led the Shirs outside to where German soldiers in gray uniforms, on foot, were gathering with others on horseback and on motorcycles. Miriam liked seeing the men in uniform. They looked handsome. But when they surrounded the family—some carrying a whip in one hand and a pistol in the other—she realized these Nazis were dangerous. Right then, she decided to act nice to them whenever the opportunity presented itself, especially to the colonel.

Carrying food and their rucksacks slung over their shoulders, the Shirs were marched into town by the soldiers. The colonel followed in his car. On the main street of the wealthier part of the bombed town, they passed apartment buildings with barely any space between them, office buildings, parks, a bakery, an Orthodox church. Soon they reached the poorer section of town where the religious Jews lived. This entire section of Buhdan Khmelnitskity Street (aka Tarashcha Street) was now fenced in with barbed wire. Ukrainian police restraining muzzled German Shepherds and Nazis wielding rifles guarded the gates along the way. Behind the fencing, disheveled Jewish men, women and children wearing armbands with a yellow Star of David were huddled by run-down houses and apartments. Miriam was horrified by these images. She figured there had to be about a thousand prisoners in the ghetto.

At the main gate, Miriam fought back tears when she saw Uncle Vladimir guarding it with another Ukrainian police officer. Then the colonel appeared and demanded the officers open the gate. He stepped inside, motioned for Aaron to enter. Aaron led the family in. When the colonel saw Miriam, he bent down and stroked her hair. He gently caressed her face. Miriam smiled. He told her that she didn't look Jewish and that if she would help him, one day he might help her. Miriam smiled again. Mania tugged at her hand and they hurried to catch up with Aaron and the rest of the family.

Mania warned Miriam not to be so nice to the Nazis. When Miriam reminded her that the colonel had said he would help her, Mania told her she was living in a fantasy world. Which was true in a way, because Miriam viewed the world as filled with awe and wonder. For her, it was a magical place. Even the Nazis could be good people, and she was determined to find a way to survive. Stardom awaited her. Little did she know how significantly her life was going to change.

CHAPTER 3

Life in the Ghetto

*F*rom growing up living a life of luxury to now sharing a small house with four families sleeping on the floor didn't upset Miriam. Somehow she felt the ghetto was special for her family. They ate well compared to the other families, mostly religious Jews from the poorest neighborhoods, because her father did rush jobs for the German soldiers and was paid in food. In her mind, the Nazis weren't that bad. The Shirs shared their wealth of food, helping everyone as much as possible. Although life was very different, Miriam still enjoyed being a child. She found that practicing her acting and singing and writing, along with indulging her curious mind, helped her fantasize away the mental distress her capture had created. Miriam didn't like working in a small room eight hours a day, sewing the yellow Jewish stars on armbands all the Jews were forced to wear, but she and the rest of the children workers were permitted to sing while they sewed. This made them happy and took their minds off their work.

Miriam often wondered what life was like beyond the fences of the ghetto. Only those who were sent out to work could see the reality of the outer world. They told stories about how badly the Nazis treated everyone, even non-Jews, because they couldn't distinguish between them by looks alone. Signs were posted everywhere proclaiming that Jews were parasites and cheaters and not to sell to Jews or hide them.

Ukrainians were continually being warned that anyone—adults

or children—communicating with Jews, hiding Jews or selling food or anything to Jews would be shot. Many mixed Jewish-Ukrainian families split up out of fear. When the Nazis questioned Ukrainian women about the whereabouts of their Jewish husbands, they threatened to kill their children if they didn't give up the information.

Guided by fear, mothers revealed where their husbands were hiding. They didn't know that, regardless of their cooperation with the Nazis, the Nazis would still take away their children younger than fifteen years old to live in a special school. There they'd be brainwashed to become Germans, forced to wear Nazi uniforms and fight in the front lines where death would come quickly to them. These children would be the first to discover any land mines, which usually decimated them. They were also the first to be shot.

Listening to the stories of the atrocities being committed against Jews made Miriam shudder. What wrongs had they committed to be punished so heinously? She didn't want to believe the stories about the Nazis' cruelty, but she couldn't ignore the truth. When she was forced to clean houses, any fantasies she had about the Nazis were destroyed. The female German soldiers demanded perfection. They shouted at the children, pushed them around, and shoved them into one another. If they discovered a miniscule imperfection, a speck of dust, the women would beat the children or whip them mercilessly with a riding crop. When Miriam witnessed a beating for the first time, she felt nauseated. She had never seen such brutality.

Police brutality became the norm in the ghetto, and Aaron worried that because Miriam looked older than the twelve years old she was, her beauty might attract the wrong kind of attention from Gestapo members who visited intermittently. He shared his concerns with Vladimir, who introduced him to some of the Ukrainian officers he was friendly with. They agreed to warn Miriam in advance of any time the Gestapo would be arriving so she could hide.

Aaron had chosen a perfect hiding place for her to scrunch up in—a weather-worn, wood-slatted rectangular crate sitting out back near the fence and several trees. The first time he showed it to Miriam and explained its importance to her, she laughed as she climbed in and out of it. After that, Aaron would periodically instruct Miriam to go in the box. He'd put the lid on and make her stay in there longer each time. Miriam decided that if hiding in the crate for a while might save her life, she was all for it.

During the weeks that passed, Aaron tormented himself trying to think of a way to get Miriam out of the ghetto. Then he remembered that Vladimir's brother and sister-in-law, who lived in a small village thirty kilometers away, had been trying to adopt a child for several years but hadn't been successful. Perhaps Vladimir could tell them he had found a Ukrainian refugee for them to adopt, and they could start the adoption process right away. If Vladimir would hide Miriam in the attic of his parents' farmhouse, she could live there until the adoption was granted. When Aaron presented his plan to Vladimir, he begged him to help Miriam escape. She had her whole life ahead of her. Vladimir agreed to help him, even though he professed fear of being found out. Aaron promised he would rather die than reveal Vladimir's role in Miriam's disappearance. He also told Vladimir he could keep everything the Shirs had entrusted to him and Pasha, as well as the family's valuable buried possessions. They decided to meet in a few days to discuss how and when they could execute their plan.

All of the prisoners in the ghetto lived in a state of shock. No semblance of normality existed. No school, no cultural events, no radio. No marriages. Run by the Ukrainian police and the Nazis, the ghetto would receive orders from the Nazis to bring Jews to clean the hospitals or pick up armbands with Jewish stars. Life in the ghetto was frightening. People would try and sneak out to sell anything they could to make money to buy bread. They risked their lives just to eat. Three boys, fifteen and sixteen years old, had the misfortune of being caught by the ghetto police outside the barbed wire fencing. As a warning to others thinking of escaping, they were beaten to death in front of everyone. Miriam almost vomited at the spectacle.

In order to survive these horrors, Miriam would recite poetry or sing and dance whenever she could. All of these things helped her feel a place of joy in her heart, no matter how disheartened she felt. But it wasn't easy.

One day the Nazis forced her to watch them torture the director of the school she had attended before the war. They made him lift and carry a huge stone. Frail from barely eating, he would take a step and drop the heavy stone. Each time he stopped, a Nazi soldier would whip him. After he could no longer lift the stone off the ground, and he lay bloody and defeated in the street, the soldier whipped him until he died. For Miriam to see this beautiful person, someone she had always looked up to, be treated so inhumanely disturbed her deeply. When she saw policemen making her teachers run while pulling a cart like a horse, and flogging them until they dropped, she broke down and cried.

Miriam couldn't believe that the Russian Jews didn't retaliate, that they couldn't run away, that they seemed so weak. She hoped the Russian army would come back to save the Jews who had been taken from their homes and stripped of their freedom. She swore if she survived she would find a way to make these horrible men pay for the violence they had perpetrated. They didn't deserve to get away with committing such atrocities.

CHAPTER 4

The Death March

After adjusting to ghetto life, Miriam and her family were informed that the Nazis had ordered all Jews be exterminated. They wondered if they would be killed too. Early one morning in December of 1941, Miriam, Aaron, Rivka, Mania and Motcyk were sleeping on the floor with three other families when they were awakened by loud banging on the door. As they jumped up to get dressed they heard soldiers shouting, "*Juden. Juden.* Come out."

They hurried outside together, holding hands. The Nazis prodded and poked them with rifles out into the street, into a line, a seemingly endless line of disheveled, emaciated Jews. The Nazis and Ukrainian police guarded them with vicious growling and barking German Shepherds. People were crying and screaming. Some were singing in Yiddish.

The soldiers and police led the thousand or so prisoners on a march through town and out into the woods. The colonel followed in his limousine, which was built to withstand the bumpy ride through the war-torn town.

Although prisoners asked the soldiers where they were being taken, the only answer they got were rifles pointed directly in their faces. What made matters worse was having to endure neighborhood Ukrainians marching alongside the Jews. Many were dressed up, some carried cameras or wine, others gave bread and salt to the guards, some took pictures of the parade of suffering humans. Miriam kept thinking these stupid people didn't know what they were doing. Rivka reassured the family that the Shirs were being resettled.

A mile deep into the woods, the soldiers marched the Jews up to a ledge thirteen kilometers above a gorge, on to a rutty, unpaved road in a graveled area between the Jewish and Orthodox Christian cemeteries. Far from town, Miriam could see nothing but trees. It was becoming clear the Nazis had no intention of resettling anyone. Miriam knew they were all going to die. The colonel ordered the Nazis and Ukrainian officers to separate the prisoners into several groups. Then they marched the first group to the edge of the ravine, where they forced the Jews to strip and kneel facing the ravine. Like the Nazi massacre in September of 1941 at the ravine in Babi Yar on the outskirts of Kiev that killed 33,771 Russian Jews—although thousands of communists, intellectuals, gypsies and enemies of the Germans were slaughtered there on other occasions—the massacre at the small Babi Yar in Tarashcha targeted Jews only.

As the Nazis took aim with their rifles and began shooting the Jews in the back of the head, they laughed at the sight of bodies being catapulted off the ledge from the force of the bullets' impact and plummeting into the natural grave below. The sounds of the gunshots, the dead bodies hitting the ground, and the screams of agony from those not lucky enough to be killed would haunt Miriam for the rest of her life. She didn't understand why nobody tried to run away. But then again, she didn't try to run either.

All of a sudden the colonel ordered the soldiers to stop their target practice. He stood in front of the group where Miriam and her family were huddled together, shaking, crying. He directed a quick glance at Miriam and winked. She could barely smile at him. When he called out Miriam's family name and that of two other families whose members were tailors, Miriam was sure they were being singled out to be killed. But as the shooting started again, the Nazis escorted the three families away from the other groups and loaded them into a security truck guarded by Ukrainian police.

The truck rumbled through the forest into town, passing by buildings plastered with posters of caricatures of Jews with big noses and long beards who were wearing *tallit*, prayer shawls. The signs quoted disparaging remarks about Jews, blaming them for food shortages, for the war, for anything that seemed to have gone wrong. Miriam knew she had to escape from this hatred. As bad as things got, she kept believing she could survive. She had to believe she could live the life she dreamed of.

When the truck finally stopped in front of a large three-story house, the soldiers shoved the nine prisoners into the beautifully decorated building and took off. Miriam observed domestic workers dusting the elegant furnishings and mopping the marble floors. She marveled at the high ceiling, the long, angled stairway to the upper floors. Quite different from the last place where the Shirs had lived in squalor, the estate offered luxury and privacy for everyone.

With the ghetto liquidated, the Nazis left the families unguarded. Aaron took charge and suggested each family claim a floor and settle into their new spaces. Miriam told her father she felt comfortable in the house, that it reminded her of home. He told her not to get used to it because he and Uncle Vladimir were working on a plan to help her escape. When he explained it to her, she protested that she didn't want to leave the family. Aaron told her it was only a matter of time until the Nazis killed them all. He encouraged her that while she still had a chance to stay alive and maybe even become a movie star, she'd better take the chance and escape to safety.

The entire family supported this decision. Rivka, Mania, and Aaron had already concurred that in order for Miriam to survive after she escaped, she would have to assume a new identity as a Ukrainian refugee whose parents had been killed in a bomb blast. Miriam protested again saying she didn't like to lie, she didn't want to lie. But Rivka suggested she think of it as an excellent opportunity to master her acting skills. Why, this could be the role of her life!

Miriam told her family the only way she'd be able to leave them, even though she considered it dangerous, was to turn this project into an adventure. She would challenge herself to be the best actress she could be. She knew if she slipped up, didn't say the right thing, she could be killed. But she was willing to take the chance, and she vowed she would one day expose the Nazis for their war crimes.

While Rivka and Mania prepared and styled a new outfit and head shawl that would make her look authentically Ukrainian, Miriam played with different names in her head. Who did she want to be? Irena, Ludmilla, Olena? She finally chose to rename herself Maria Nesterenko. During the next few months she'd occasionally wrap the shawl around her head like Ukrainian women and girls did and wear the outfit for short periods to accustom herself to her new image. She'd walk around hearing her story in her head. "My name is Maria Nesterenko. I'm a Ukrainian refugee. My parents were killed in a bomb raid and I'm all alone." She had to convince herself that she was Maria Nesterenko, not Miriam Shir. Afraid she might talk in her sleep about her past, Miriam repeated her story every night in bed until she drifted off to sleep. Even so, she was haunted in her dreams with images of the horrors she had witnessed.

Things were going well for the three families, the only remaining Jews in Tarashcha. The colonel used the men to provide for the Nazis' blacksmith and tailoring needs, which kept the men alive. Every once in a while Miriam would enjoy some brief attention from the handsome colonel. She wondered when he was going to ask her for help, when he was going to help her like he had told her the first time they met.

One late afternoon in September of 1942, Aaron and Vladimir were sitting in the Shirs' living room drinking vodka and celebrating Vladimir's news that his brother and sister-in-law had completed their application to adopt Maria Nesterenko. The paperwork would be processed and approved within three months. Aaron told Vladimir he believed the Nazis might spare the families because the colonel let them come and go as they pleased, which would make it relatively easy to sneak Miriam out. Vladimir agreed that they could help her escape, but insisted Aaron was wrong about the families being spared. The colonel was being transferred to Kiev and would be leaving shortly. He would have no say in saving the three remaining families. And since Hitler's Final Solution, the death sentence for all Jews, had now been fully implemented, no Jews could be allowed to live. A million had already been murdered. Aaron heeded Vladimir's words and convinced him they needed to move Miriam immediately. Vladimir promised to pick her up with his horse and carriage at ten o'clock that night.

CHAPTER 5

The Journey to Freedom

*L*ater that evening the Shirs gathered around Miriam. Dressed in her Ukrainian clothing and head scarf, she cried as her mother impressed upon her the importance of respecting the people who would adopt her after she stayed at Uncle Vladimir's parents' attic. Rivka advised her to sweep, wash dishes, do whatever chores these country folk needed her to do. Mania encouraged her to act like the brave women she admired in movies. Miriam posed with her hands on her hips and quoted Homer's advice to go forth with a spirit that feared nothing. One day she would tell the world about the cruel Nazis.

As ten o'clock drew near, Miriam slung her rucksack packed with her few pieces of clothing over her shoulder. She kissed everyone goodbye, adjusted her shawl. Straightening herself up to her full height, she stepped out into the cool night air just as Uncle Vladimir arrived. She hurried to the carriage and climbed in. Vladimir crossed himself, pulled on the reins, and off they went. It took half an hour to reach his parents' home in a rural area outside of Tarashcha. Vladimir instructed Miriam to be quiet while he maneuvered the carriage around to the back of a small A-frame house with a barn just across the back yard. He didn't want to wake the nearby neighbors. No one could know he was hiding a Jewish child.

In the dark of night, Vladimir guided Miriam to a ladder propped against the house that extended to a second-story attic. He helped her get her footing on the first rung, gave her a gentle nudge and climbed the ladder behind her. When she stopped at the entrance to the attic, Vladimir reached around her and pushed the small door open.

Miriam balked at the dimly lit space. She had to crawl in because there wasn't enough room between the floor and the ceiling for her to stand— she could only sit or lie down on the floor covered with hay.

Miriam in her disguise as Ukrainian Maria Nesterenko

Vladimir told her she should use the pillow and blankets he had provided to make herself comfortable. She could relieve herself with the nearby bucket. He promised her that his father would bring her food and a fresh bucket for her bodily functions every day. He apologized about the poor conditions she would have to endure until the adoption papers were approved. He told her he wished she could live in the house, but if anyone suspected his parents were hiding her, they'd all be shot.

Before Miriam went to sleep that night she crossed herself like she'd seen Uncle Vladimir and other Ukrainians do. Since it seemed her God had abandoned her, she thought maybe the Christian God would help her. She felt so alone that she didn't care which God she asked for help. All she wanted was her "mommy."

Twice a day, in the darkness of morning and evening, Vladimir's father climbed the ladder to give Miriam bread and soup and potatoes through the small entry door. But she had to share her food with the rats that had learned the feeding schedule. She found it easier to befriend them than be frightened of them as they waited alongside her to be fed. After all, they were very much like her, for they too had to depend on the forces of nature to survive. They had to use their instincts to know who would help them and who would hurt them. So did Miriam.

About three weeks after her arrival, Miriam decided she would sneak into the barn before the sun came up. She was sure the chickens that squawked every morning had laid eggs, and she wanted some. Shivering in the cold darkness, she carefully descended the ladder. She hurried into the barn where the chickens were pecking around and removed their eggs from their nests. After she sucked them raw from the shells, she buried the eggshells outside in the dirt and hurried back to the attic.

For the next two months, Miriam ate eggs at least twice a week. She managed to stay healthy, probably because the nutritious raw eggs strengthened her immune system. Or maybe, she thought, God was helping her. The more often she repeated her refugee story to herself in this tiny room, the more she started to believe in God. Now she crossed herself several times a day.

On the pre-dawn morning Vladimir sneaked Miriam out of the attic to transport her to his brother's, Miriam looked lovely in her traditional Ukrainian garb. Nervous and excited to meet her new parents, she missed her own parents and wondered if she'd ever see them again.

Miriam treasured the thirty-kilometer carriage ride in the crisp air to the small country village of Chapiewka. When Vladimir introduced Miriam as Maria Nesterenko to his brother and sister-in-law, they both hugged her, then ushered them into a small dining area. At the table, her new mother uttered a prayer thanking Jesus and the guardian angels for saving Maria Nesterenko and bringing her to them. They shared meat, potatoes, bread and soup. Then Vladimir stood to leave. He hugged Miriam and held her for a few moments. As she kissed her precious friend goodbye, her eyes filled with tears.

It took a while for Miriam to accustom herself to the disciplined, structured life her adoptive parents imposed on her. Instead of going to school, she worked at home all day milking cows, cleaning the pigs' sty, scrubbing floors. She helped the mother bake bread and did whatever else she asked Miriam to do.

As long as Miriam finished all her chores, she was allowed to play with the neighborhood girls who came to see her after school. She taught them poems, sang with them, helped direct them to put on short plays in the yard. When her mother took her to a dress shop downtown, the owner told Miriam she was so beautiful she could be a movie star. That was all Miriam had to hear to reignite her dream, although she was beginning to doubt it would ever come true.

For the next six months Miriam lived in safety with no sign of the Nazis anywhere. The actress she had aspired to become had convinced the townspeople she was Ukrainian. They accepted her, never imagining she was from Jewish stock. She liked her adoptive parents, her simple life, yet she longed to see her real family. She wanted to gaze into her mother's soft warm eyes, hold Mania's little boy, melt into her father's arms. She thought about her family as she went to sleep at night, but her dreams seemed always to resolve into nightmares of whips and guns by morning.

Meanwhile, in the Tarashcha ghetto, the Shirs learned that the Nazis were returning from Kiev with a special order to enforce the Final Solution and kill the remaining three Jewish families. Knowing Vladimir could no longer jeopardize his family's safety to save them, Aaron told Mania she had to prepare to escape with two-and-a-half-year-old Motyck later that night. He gave her directions to Vladimir's brother's home, instructing her to beg for food so he would let them in. If she got inside the house, he wanted her to pretend she didn't know Miriam and wait until they were alone to inform Miriam that Aaron and Rivka were alive. Mania had a friend who would hide her and her son for the night before she began the trek to find Miriam. At eleven in the evening, Mania and Motyck kissed the family good-bye and walked away from the estate.

The next day, when Aaron and Rivka had occasion to pass the police station, they couldn't help but notice the tailors out front, dirtied from head to toe, digging what appeared to be a large grave. Aaron didn't like that they were suddenly being guarded by the Ukrainian police and a Gestapo officer. Assuming something must be wrong, he slipped his arm through Rivka's, hurried her along past them. But before they got very far they were stopped by the colonel. He asked for Miriam, whom he hadn't seen since his transfer to Kiev, and he told the Shirs he would follow them home to say hello to her and their daughter-in-law. When Rivka responded that the girls were off playing somewhere, he instructed the Shirs to turn around and go with him to the police station.

On the run with her son, Mania found her way to Miriam's adoptive family's home. When the father opened the door, he was surprised to see a very Jewish-looking woman with a prominent nose and dark hair and eyes with her little boy. Mania looked at him pleadingly and begged for food. The wife appeared, stepped outside and glanced around to see if anyone was watching and hurried them inside. She led them to the breakfast table where Miriam was eating. When Miriam looked up, she gulped, but showed no sign of recognizing Mania. Mania introduced herself as if she didn't know Miriam either. But her son recognized Miriam and ran to her and hugged her. Instantly her adoptive parents questioned her. Who was this woman? Was she Jewish? Was Miriam Jewish? After Miriam answered their questions, they insisted she would have to go home. Mania told them Miriam couldn't return to Tarashcha because her parents had been killed. But as much as the couple loved Miriam, they said they couldn't risk being caught with a Jewish child living in their home. They assured Miriam she would be safe. If they hadn't recognized her as being Jewish, probably no one else would either.

Once Miriam packed her rucksack and goodbyes had been said, Miriam, Mania and Motyck walked to a nearby abandoned park. Mania told Miriam that a friend with an inside source had informed her the morning after she ran from the ghetto how the colonel had questioned Miriam's parents about her and Miriam's whereabouts. He didn't believe they didn't know where to find the girls.

When Miriam heard how the Nazis had mercilessly beaten her parents until they died, she couldn't fight back the tears. Her heart ached over the tragedy of their death and the drama her life had become. But she still had to survive. There was no time for tears. They had to decide which direction to set out on. Mania told Miriam if they stayed together and the Germans caught them, they'd know from Motyck's circumcision that they were Jewish and would kill them all. Therefore, since Miriam had the best chance of surviving, Mania convinced her to strike out on her own. Someone had to live to tell the world about the cruelty of the Nazis so it would never happen again.

With tears in her eyes, sobbing softly, Miriam walked off in one direction. Mania and her son set out in another direction. Miriam didn't know what fate awaited her. She decided to keep her faith and take things as they came. Of course, she hoped Mania and her son would survive, even though she doubted they would. She couldn't know then that in the spring of 1943, when Mania would be working in the fields, she'd be recognized by an old boyfriend who used to frequent the movie theatre where she sold tickets. An agricultural consultant who taught the Germans how to produce better crops, he told her he wanted to help her and her son. Mania didn't trust him because she knew he worked with the Germans, but when he offered to take them to safety, she accepted his offer. Exhausted, she and her son slept through the carriage ride. They were awakened by Ukrainian police shouting, pulling them out of the carriage and dragging them into the police station. Next came the interrogation about Miriam's whereabouts. Every time Mania said she didn't know where Miriam was, an officer beat her with a club. Mania's "friend" had turned her in to the authorities. The authorities pummeled Mania and Motyck to death.

It was picking season, a few months before winter. Miriam, who looked older than her fourteen years, walked all day looking for work, passing through farms and stopping to eat whatever food she could find growing. At night she climbed onto a small haystack in a field and lay down to gaze at the stars and the moon. So many thoughts ran through her mind. Would she ever be able to go home again? What would her life be like when she got there? Was there any hope she could pursue her acting career? A peal of thunder interrupted her thoughts, and Miriam decided to read it as a positive sign. She felt good to be sleeping under the moonlight.

The next morning Miriam continued her journey until she found work in a small village. As a Ukrainian war refugee and orphan, she didn't need identification papers, and although picking potatoes and beets all day blistered her hands, Miriam was thankful for the food and shelter she received as pay. Soon she felt safe again.

But after she'd been working for about a month, suddenly the Nazis marched into town. They ordered the girls in the field to line up and announced they would be moving those sixteen years or older to Germany to work in a factory. Although the German soldiers called the Ukrainians *"farfluchte,"* dirty swine, the Ukrainians didn't object. They knew there was no future picking in the fields. Like Miriam, they thought it might be exciting to go to Germany, to start over again and make a decent wage.

When the soldiers asked for a show of hands from those sixteen and older, Miriam raised her hand. She wanted to meet the good Germans, see another country, and live in a place where no one knew her. But when the Nazis told the girls they'd be taken to the Nazis' administrative center in Tarashcha to be processed for documentation papers, Miriam knew she'd be recognized by the police there. They'd never send her to Germany to work. They would kill her. So, she packed her rucksack and ran off in the middle of the night.

Miriam walked all night. In the morning, she passed several farms until she ended up in the village of Stavyshche, an administrative center the Nazis had not yet invaded. When she noticed a group of people gathered outside a mansion, she made her way over to them and asked for help finding work. They told her she had come to the right place—the building served as a city hall and employment center—and that people traveled to this big village because it offered more job opportunities than smaller villages. With her status as a Ukrainian refugee and orphan, they assured her she would easily get a job working in the fields.

The fieldworkers Miriam befriended on the job, mostly women and children, lived together in a big house. They liked Miriam and made her feel at home.

Every Saturday they invited her to join them in church. As part of the service, the priest would ask different people to read from the scriptures. None of the parishioners could read very well, not even the priest. So when Miriam was called on and read flawlessly and effortlessly, everyone fell in love with her. The former "A" student who hadn't completed the fifth grade outshined them all, and the priest bestowed the honor of official church reader on her. Miriam particularly liked this religious sect, which may have been Jehovah's Witnesses, because members refused to join the military or align with Hitler. Politically neutral, they celebrated Sabbath on Saturday like the Jews, not on Sunday like other Christians.

These evangelists considered Miriam a blessing, an angel sent from heaven to pass on the words of God. They were a blessing for her too. The church fed her and protected her, especially from advances of the boys and men that she charmed at town dances she attended with her friends. The more beautifully she read in church, the more she thrived. It felt good to be appreciated, to feel safe. But even though she looked and dressed like the other Ukrainian girls, and had practically come to believe she wasn't Jewish, Miriam always feared someone would recognize her. She worried that if she talked in her sleep she might say something about her past that could endanger her. And so she found great solace in praying to this non-Jewish God to help her return home to Tarashcha.

Miriam enjoyed her peaceful life in Stavyshche for more than a year. Then one day in December of 1944 she heard the roar of German planes and artillery overhead. As the aircraft dropped bombs, Miriam ran to a community cellar with her friends. The shelter, equipped with cots and blankets and minimal lighting, housed some fifty people. For a day and a night the strafing continued, which made sleeping difficult.

When the noise finally subsided, Miriam swore she could hear men outside speaking Russian. They had been drinking and were using harsh words, speaking true Russian, not Ukrainian-Russian. Eager to talk to them, she scrambled up out of the cellar. Her eyes teared as much from the smoke billowing out of bombed houses and shops as from the sense of joy she expe-

Miriam hiding as Maria and a friend, 1944

rienced at the sight of soldiers from the Russian army stationed nearby. She heard one of them make a wolf whistle at her and stretched herself up to her full height. Just as she assumed her favorite pose with her feet spread and hands on her hips, a handsome lieutenant approached her. Miriam's heart skipped several beats.

The lieutenant introduced himself. He told Miriam she looked tired, asked if she was okay and how he could help her. After she explained that her family had been killed and she had been in hiding for two-and-a-half years, Miriam broke down crying. The Lieutenant gently pulled her into his chest to console her. He let her sob until she quieted down and released herself from his hold.

Then she slipped her shawl off her head and shook her hair free. It felt good to be her real self, to feel alive again. She told the lieutenant she had changed her identity in order to survive after escaping from the ghetto, and he commended her on how successfully she had managed to convince everyone she was a Ukrainian refugee.

She chalked it up to her years of experience acting in the shtetl. She even confided that she had wanted to be a movie star, but now all she wanted to do was go home to Tarashcha so she could continue her studies.

He informed her the war was still going on, but the Russian army had forced the Germans out of Tarashcha. Miriam asked if he could take her home. Unfortunately, the direction he was leading his men would only get her halfway to Tarashcha. She would have to travel alone for two more days on foot. Miriam trusted her sense of adventure to complete this last part of her journey. And with the lieutenant's commitment to draw her a map and provide her with food and water, she foresaw herself bringing this horrific chapter in her life to an end.

Later in the day the lieutenant sent word to Miriam that a car would come and take her to the Russian military camp to stay the night so she'd be ready to leave with the men before dawn. She and the soldiers spent most of the evening playing cards, laughing a lot at jokes the lieutenant told. Then it was lights out. They all needed plenty of rest before they began their trek in the wee hours of the morning.

While Miriam and the lieutenant traveled together in a horse-drawn carriage for a few days with the soldiers following in wagons, the lieutenant asked her to tell him what her life had been like in Tarashcha and how she had managed to survive in hiding after escaping.

She reminisced about the good times—her musical shows, the gypsy summers—happy to be recalling them. But she had more difficulty talking about the war and some of the horrible tortures she had to endure watching in the ghetto. Occasionally she would cry, and he would rest his hand on hers to soothe her. By the time she finished her stories, the horses were slowing to a stop.

The lieutenant, amazed by Miriam's fortitude and determination, praised her for her courage. He told her she was a hero, that the war was over for her now. As far as he was concerned, she should go home and follow her dream to become a movie star.

Miriam, once so devoted to that dream, doubted it could ever come true. With her parents dead, and no way to know where her brother Simeon in the Marines and Aleksandr in the Army were, she was going to have to take care of herself. It would be hard enough to complete her education and hopefully work as a teacher, let alone embark on an acting career. Perhaps Uncle Vladimir and Aunt Pasha could help her—if they were still alive.

The lieutenant pulled the map he had drawn out of his pocket, shared it with Miriam. He showed her the route she would have to follow—no winding roads, just straight paths with minimal directional changes—which seemed fairly simple to Miriam. She immediately reveled in a renewed sense of faith.

Miriam buttoned up her worn coat and wrapped her shawl around her head to keep her warm. It was time for her to make the rest of the trip alone. If there was a God, she wondered, would he guide her home? She decided she had to believe some guardian angel was watching over her for she had come this far, so very close to home.

As the lieutenant helped her out of the carriage, Miriam stepped down into the snow in her flimsy canvas shoes. He held her in his arms; he seemed to not want to let her go, and he kissed her.

Miriam brushed away her tears. She thanked him for being her guardian angel and turned to part ways. She looked up at the cloudless blue sky that illuminated the snow-laden trees at the edge of the forest. Then she set off for home.

The lieutenant watched her walk away, her rucksack gently bouncing against her back, her feet sinking into the snow with every step, a lonely figure in the snowy glimmering woods.

CHAPTER 6

Miriam's New Life

Miriam sang as she trekked through the snow-covered ground. She felt no fear, except she worried she might have gotten pregnant from the lieutenant's kiss. That's how little she knew about sex. And every so often along her way she would jump up and down several times with hopes of aborting.

Even though Miriam didn't quite know where she was, she kept looking for the guideposts the lieutenant had pointed out to her, following his every instruction. By the time she grew tired near the end of the day, she had covered more than half the distance to Tarashcha. She told herself it didn't matter that her feet were wet and swollen. It didn't matter she was chilled to the bone. She, Miriam Shir, and her alter ego Maria Nesterenko, had managed to escape certain death from Hitler's Final Solution. Maybe the lieutenant was right. Maybe she was a hero. But in her mind she wouldn't be a hero until the day she could do something to make the Nazis pay for their crimes. First and foremost, though, she had to get home.

When Miriam arrived in Tarashcha twenty-four hours later, she found herself at the deserted gypsy camp she had so many fond memories of. Tired, dazed, practically frozen, she rubbed her numb hands together and exhaled a vapory breath. Tears ran down her face. She gazed at the brilliant blue sky and crossed herself. Probably it would be best to stop at Vladimir and Pasha's house first. They would care for her until she felt strong enough to live alone in the big Shir home.

Aunt Pasha couldn't believe her eyes when Miriam showed up at her door, still the beautiful Miriam she remembered, but much thinner. After hugging and kissing and crying, the two went inside and sat by the fire in the living room. Pasha fluffed the pillows on the divan for Miriam to lie down. She helped her off with her shoes, a bit startled by her red swollen feet and ankles, and covered her with a blanket. When Miriam asked for Vladimir, Pasha told her that he had been murdered for helping her escape. She stressed that Miriam shouldn't worry about it because he had been sick, and thanks to him taking her far enough away, Miriam had been spared. She was the sole Jewish survivor in Tarashcha.

For the next few weeks Aunt Pasha fed Miriam and bathed her in the *balia*. Whenever she attempted to engage her in conversation about the war, Miriam would tell her she wanted to forget what happened, and she didn't want to talk about it ever again. It was like a bad dream, a nightmare that kept recurring. She just wanted to find her brothers and resume her life.

Aunt Pasha did whatever necessary to help Miriam and gained approval from the Russian government for Miriam to move back into the Shir estate. But Miriam didn't want to be alone in the big house. Nobody was there. No family. No workers. No animals. No nothing. Which was no problem, according to Aunt Pasha. She introduced Miriam to Marisa, a young Polish refugee two years older than Miriam whose family had been killed in a bombing. She lived alone in a nearby village and welcomed the idea of moving in with Miriam.

Marisa and Miriam became fast friends. With the help of neighbors who carted the Shirs' furniture Aunt Pasha had been storing back to the estate, the two teenagers set up residence. They visited

Miriam (left) and Marisa, 1945

City Hall regularly where the Red Cross gave out clothes and packages with food. Sometimes they would stand in the food line, Miriam daydreaming about the chocolate she would soon be savoring. Sometimes they waited for clothes. She enjoyed wearing the green coat she received through the American Red Cross from an unknown American. And when she stood in front of the mirror using her finger to apply the toothpaste that came with no toothbrush, she marveled at how the Americans lived. Before the war she had put baking soda on her finger to clean her teeth and massage her gums.

Miriam missed her family very much. It saddened her to know she would never see her parents again. And being back in her home reignited the dreams of the horrors of the Nazi occupation. But when she learned that a few Jews who had evacuated Tarascha before the Germans marched in had come back and were going to dig up her parents' bones from the grave in front of the police station and put them in the small Babi Yar ravine, she felt proud.

Soon she learned that the post office was holding letters from her brothers who had been looking for her during her years in hiding. She collected her mail and read it, feeling blessed her brothers were alive. They had sent money in every letter, which would help make her new life a little easier. Her brother Simeon also sent books and clothes. Both brothers in their letters urged her to go back to school. She hadn't been able to finish fifth grade because of the war. They knew how smart she was. And they knew how important it was for her to be well educated.

Encouraged by their advice, Miriam excelled on a reading test at school. She received credit for the grades she had missed and was admitted to seventh grade. She went to work in a nursery school after school as a teacher's assistant. As soon as she became accustomed to this routine, she added nursing school at night to her busy schedule. Education and work consumed her, and she loved it!

Not long after Miriam corresponded with her brothers, the Army gave her youngest brother Aleksandr a special leave for five days. The tall, blond, blue-eyed Shir arrived in Tarashcha the end of January, 1945, to help Miriam with repairs the family home needed. He also contacted officials to find the police officers who had absconded with some of the family's belongings and requested they return the property to the Shirs.

Aleksandr believed Miriam was too young to live alone with Marisa without a man around, and it concerned him. He had been gone from home so long that he didn't know any men available to court his sister. So when he was introduced to a handsome, successful Jewish man his age from Poland who lived down the street, he told Miriam he wanted to introduce him to her. She refused. She claimed

Miriam and her brother Aleksandr, 1945

her independence mattered more to her than a man. She wanted to be self-sufficient. But Aleksandr threatened to cut his stay short unless she promised to meet Aaron before Aleksandr went back to the Army, or would at least promise to meet him soon. Miriam agreed.

Aleksandr's visit lightened Miriam's spirit. She appreciated his help and caring of her. She felt fortunate that the Russian government was very good to her also. The whole town treated her well because they admired her bravery. But conditions were difficult. Food was scarce. Just as before the war, there was no running water or toilet and Miriam had to carry buckets to the well whenever she needed water. She had to boil towels or use leaves to clean herself if she used the outhouse. Still, no hardship could compare to the pain, anguish and suffering she and so many others had been subjected to.

Life for Miriam had changed dramatically. In addition to losing her family, all of her childhood Jewish friends were dead too. She still loved to read and fantasize about her life, so she spent as much time as she could in the library. She devoured books, especially romantic novels. And she dreamt of meeting a handsome, Jewish, Russian officer, a man with a good education who would romance her. After all, when she turned sixteen in a few months she'd be considered an adult, old enough to apply for a passport and travel. Maybe she'd take a train somewhere to explore a nearby town or big city and fall in love with a stranger. Although she soon met a young man in Tarashcha whom she developed feelings for, nothing came of it.

Every day on her way to school Miriam passed the house of the man from Poland she had promised her brother she would meet. One afternoon when she was walking home, his housekeeper approached her and told her Aaron was looking forward to meeting her, as her brother had suggested.

Aaron Gopman was born in the village of Vishnevets, Poland, in

1919. As a result of the village being annexed to Russia, Aaron had to serve in the Russian Army from 1939 to 1944. He was wounded and hospitalized several times, including once for frostbite. While serving on the front line because he was Jewish, he was forced to search for land mines using his hands. Luck had been with him for several years until a mine exploded and blew off the first three fingers of his right hand. That ended his military career.

Miriam in 1946

After he recovered from his war injuries, the Communist Party sent Aaron to Tarashcha to act as a director for a government distribution center brokering meat and food citizens had submitted as payment for their taxes. He performed his job well, and the Russians accepted Aaron as a Polish Jew.

Ten years her senior, Aaron Gopman was the first man in Miriam's life. Well-known and respected by the community, generous, kind, and understanding, he taught her about many things, including necking. His position at the distribution center gave him access to substantial amounts of food, especially chicken and eggs, from which he gifted Miriam and Marisa.

Shortly after they started dating, Aaron made a beautiful party for Miriam's sixteenth birthday. He invited neighbors and workers and the rabbi to his home. Marisa was there too. Everyone drank vodka and danced and laughed. Miriam had so much fun, she wished she hadn't waited so long to get to know Aaron. And when he sang to her in Polish, Jewish and Russian, she loved it. But the more he showed Miriam he cared, the more he supplied hard-to-get food and offered Miriam money, the less interested she became. She would even go out of her way to avoid passing his house on the off chance she might run into him.

Aaron felt different about their relationship. He had lived through difficult times, and the war years had taken a toll on him. Miriam brought him back to life. She made him happy, and he wanted to marry her and take care of her. Miriam wouldn't hear of it. She planned to graduate from the tenth grade, which was equivalent to a high school diploma, in two years. She would then enroll in a special course to become a kindergarten teacher.

Miriam confided in Marisa about her relationship with Aaron because she knew Marisa had experience with men. That was when she learned she had to do a lot more than kiss to get pregnant! But men had taken advantage of Marisa, so she taught Miriam to not trust Aaron, to protect herself. Yet when Miriam would tell her that she wasn't interested in Aaron, that she didn't want to get married because she wanted to pursue her education and become a teacher, Marisa would reply he was so nice, so handsome, such a good catch. And she would question Miriam about why she couldn't commit to a relationship with him.

It soon became apparent that Marisa was falling in love with Aaron. Whenever he came to the house for a date with Miriam, Marisa would openly flirt with him. Miriam didn't like the jealousy Marisa's infatuation aroused in her. After a few incidents, Miriam told Marisa she loved Aaron. She just didn't want to marry him. She didn't feel grown up enough at sixteen to be ready for a marriage, which Marisa couldn't understand. In response, Marisa said she wanted to marry Aaron and take him home to Poland with her. Now, faced with the thought of Marisa possibly taking Aaron away from her, Miriam dealt with her jealousy by spending more time with Aaron.

A few weeks before the war ended in May of 1945, the military center in Tarashcha delivered a telegram to Miriam. As she read that Simeon's ship had struck a mine and all the marines on board had died, she burst into tears. For her this was the worst thing that could happen because she loved him dearly. She had already lost her oldest brother Emile who was killed in the war in Finland in 1940, his wife and son, and her parents. Now only she and Aleksandr remained in the family.

Miriam and Aaron had been dating for more than a year when Aaron again asked Miriam to marry him and have a family together. This time, she gave the idea great consideration. Life on her own had become difficult going to school and working, and Miriam felt guilty accepting food and money from Aaron. If she married him, it would make her an honest woman. Her brother Aleksandr had moved to Kiev and offered to let her sell the Shir estate. So, partially in order to please her brother and friends who believed a beautiful young girl should have a husband, and partially because she knew the time had come for her to give up her independence, she agreed.

In April of 1946, Miriam married Aaron. She was seventeen years old and Aaron was twenty-seven. They moved into the duplex Miriam bought with the money from the sale of the estate. It was a modern building with electricity, a well, trees and two patches of untilled earth. When Miriam got pregnant three months later, Marisa left for Poland. From there she wrote Miriam that she planned to move to Israel, where many Jews were migrating. But the government's censorship laws prohibited Miriam from writing to her, so they lost touch with one another.

Miriam and Aaron as newlyweds, 1946

Miriam finished school and became a teacher. She stopped working just in time to deliver her son Martin on May 22, 1947. No one performed the usual circumcision for fear it could create problems for the family. Because Aaron worked for the Communist Party, and it was common knowledge that he was Jewish, the Party sent a comrade to make sure the boy had not been circumcised. Miriam was stunned when the woman removed Martin's blanket and inspected his private area. She dreamed of freedom.

Aaron earned a good living and was very generous with Miriam. She appreciated his love and kind ways, but he couldn't give her what she wanted. And she suffered from the lack of passion she longed for. Ever the romantic, she continued reading romantic novels—Anna Karenina by Tolstoy was one of her favorites—imagining what it would be like to meet a well-educated man who would romance her.

Miriam (back right) and other teachers, late 1940s

Although she didn't foresee having a love affair like Anna Karenina, she could understand how it could happen. She was tired of her husband taking her for granted.

As soldiers slowly started returning from the war, Miriam and her husband got together with other young Jewish people who had migrated to Tarashcha. The prevalent antisemitism seemed to bond them to one another more than ever before. Collectively, they had lost so many family members that they became family to one another.

With a resurgence of Judaism, observation of the Sabbath and Jewish life gave meaning to their lives. Aaron, who knew the Torah by heart, took to reciting passages with friends at Sabbath dinners. No longer was it shameful to be Jewish. Jews were going to Kiev, Moscow, Leningrad, anywhere they could to study and catch up on the education they had missed. Many became engineers, doctors, lawyers.

During the war Miriam was aware only of her own experience.

She didn't know that the Russians had invaded Poland and made a pact with Hitler, who had been moving through Europe country by country. Hitler had promised Stalin peace with Russia if he could take part of Poland and let Russia have the other part. Stalin agreed. Miriam didn't know that Stalin was killing thousands of people, even his own generals, and that when Hitler came to Russia the Russians had to strengthen their military forces. Nor did she know Churchill made Roosevelt understand that the United States needed to help Russia defeat Germany. She didn't know about the concentration camps in Germany and Poland until she saw film footage of them after the war ended.

The movies about the war made Miriam ill. She and her friends would scream from seeing the emaciated Jewish bodies, the dead Jewish bodies, the Nazi soldiers. With the advent of TV, news of the disasters spread quickly. Extermination camps were everywhere except Holland. There the Jews had been enslaved in work camps, and the underground press had printed 300,000 Jewish stars inscribed with the words "Jews and non-Jews are one and the same." Reports that the Germans had made soap and lampshades from the bodies of the exterminated Jews sickened everyone.

Miriam had gone through hell to survive, but the concentration camps were worse than she could have imagined. Now she was certain she had been chosen to survive so she could tell the world about the horrors of the war. She could help to make sure nothing like this would happen again, and she would seek justice against the Nazi war criminals for their crimes against humanity.

CHAPTER 7

Communism

$\mathcal{T}$he Russians appreciated America's efforts through the American Red Cross to send clothes and food during the war. They even named streets after famous Americans, including Eleanor Roosevelt. They believed Americans were lucky because the war wasn't being fought on American soil. Through the eyes of the average Russian, Americans lived like kings and queens. In Russia if someone wanted an unobtainable product, people would say,

Miriam, 1946

"What do you think, you're in America?" "What do you expect? You're not in America. You're in Russia."

Unfortunately, within a year after the end of the war, the Communist Party stepped up its anti-American propaganda. In addition to antisemitism, another form of hatred had emerged. Working on a non-stop basis to undermine American aid and promote suspicion of America, the communists accused Americans of entering the war too late. They claimed Americans were now sending packages to Russia because they felt guilty for letting the Russians do so much of the fighting while they lived the good life. They also criticized capitalism. How could it be fair for some people to be rich, they reasoned, while others were so poor they had to sell their organs or eyes.

At the same time Russians were being brainwashed about the merits of communism and the pitfalls of the American way of life, many Russian families were receiving packages of clothes and money from family members living in the United States. When Miriam saw photos of Aaron's family in America standing by a fancy car, everyone dressed up, bedazzled with jewelry, she realized the government had been lying to the people. America looked pretty good to her. When, before her wedding, she received a ten-dollar bill from Aaron's grandmother's sister in the States—which she thought was a fortune—she stuffed it in a bottle and buried it in the outhouse for safekeeping.

While America was the target of hate, soon the propaganda against the Jews began again. Although pogroms had been part of Russian history before the war, the Communist Party declared pogroms no longer existed and that the government, along with the American government, was helping Israel to become a state. The Communists told the Jews that everyone was equal and it was every Russian's duty to become patriotic about communism. Even the children were force-fed communist propaganda through songs.

When Israel won its independence as a state—after being attacked by the Arabs in 1948 in the Six Day War and taking Sinai from Egypt and the Golan Heights from Syria—the Russian Jews danced in the streets. They were proud of the Israelis. This new breed of Jews had fought hard and won their independence. But the rest of the population blamed the Jews for the spread of disease and food shortages and for just about everything else wrong in the country. Influenced by Social Realism that produced empty propaganda, even the Jews started to believe that Jews were bad. When the Russian government denounced the Polish Jews, claiming they were in Russia temporarily to destroy the government, the Jewish community feared Stalin might create another Holocaust. Miriam feared it too, and she wasn't surprised in the 1950s when Stalin's government imprisoned the "Cosmopolitans," the Polish and Russian Jews who comprised the intelligentsia of writers, poets, doctors, teachers, high level managers.

CHAPTER 8

Aaron's Imprisonment

Miriam felt secure that Aaron would be spared from the government's crackdown on Polish Jews. He had received many medals while serving in the Russian army, and the Russian government recognized his hard work by moving his rank up to manager at his job. But one evening in November of 1951, the MGB (which became the KGB in 1954) showed up at the Gopman home and handcuffed Aaron on grounds that he was a Polish spy sent to undermine the government. Much to Miriam's horror, they ransacked the house searching for papers and documents.

When one of the agents uncovered a ledger with names, he held it up to Aaron and accused him of anti-Soviet activities. He charged that Aaron had been giving information to these people named. Aaron laughed. He asked the agent how records he kept for the government that listed taxpayers and the taxes they paid could be used to convict him of spying. That was the last thing Miriam heard before the MGB pulled him up out of his chair and whisked him away.

The Russians imprisoned Aaron in Tarashcha as a Polish spy. Soon they moved him to a larger city, to the Bialia Cercova, the White Church, where they left him to rot in solitary confinement for two months. During the week and on weekends Miriam brought food to the big jail at MGB headquarters. The guards would accept the food for Aaron but wouldn't allow her to see or speak to him. On one of her visits she was told that Aaron had been moved to a political jail, the whereabouts of which could not be disclosed.

Now Miriam had no idea where to find Aaron. Frantic, she searched for him, unsuccessfully, for eight months while he was under investigation. She didn't know what to think. She didn't know if he was alive or dead. Then she received a notice that he was going to be tried as a Zionist political prisoner. Under pressure from the beatings he received, Aaron had admitted to the MGB that as a leader for youth in Poland he helped prepare them to go to Palestine to fight for Israel.

Miriam knew she had to seek legal counsel if she wanted to help Aaron. In order to hire the best attorney from Moscow, Miriam had to sell everything she could—clothes, shoes, furniture, anything and everything. Almost penniless, she managed to get by because she worked as a kindergarten teacher at the school her son Martin attended, which fed them three meals a day.

At the trial, it didn't matter that Aaron had been awarded medals for his exemplary service in the Russian army for five years or that he was the only Polish soldier to be so decorated. What mattered was his past. The government brought witnesses from Poland to testify against Aaron. And although Aaron insisted on his innocence as a young boy teaching Zionism to children in Poland, he couldn't convince the court. Aaron's attorney explained that Aaron's activities were not a crime in Poland at the time he was a Zionist. He insisted on Aaron's allegiance to the Russians. How could he be a traitor or a spy when he had fought so valiantly in the Russian army against the Germans and worked so hard to help the Russian government? But his words fell on deaf ears. The Russian government was determined to try Aaron as a spy, even though no proof existed to justify the claim.

When Aaron's verdict was handed down in December of 1952,

Miriam felt relieved he didn't receive the maximum sentence of twenty-five years of hard labor in Siberia. Most inmates given such a sentence were shot immediately. But his sentencing of twenty years seemed an eternity to wait for him. She couldn't imagine how he would survive in Siberia where the average subarctic temperature was below zero. Nor could she visualize how she could support herself and Martin by herself. Still, she was pleased the attorney had saved her husband's life. Although Miriam knew life alone with a son would be difficult, and her young friends were dating, the thought of divorcing Aaron never entered her mind. He was the father of her child.

CHAPTER 9

Miriam's Life without Aaron

Only twenty-three years old, Miriam returned to her teaching career. She saved every bit of money she could. When the MGB decided that half of Miriam's duplex belonged to Aaron, the government confiscated everything in his half of the house. Miriam and Martin were forced to live in one room with use of the kitchen. The other half of the house was rented to a couple she didn't know. Although Miriam felt victimized by this arrangement, it turned out in her best interest because the husband and wife took care of Martin whenever Miriam needed help.

Soon after Aaron was found guilty and sent to a forced labor camp of the Gulag in Siberia, a special MGB agency designated to protect children of families of political prisoners routinely sent a car to take Miriam to headquarters, two to three times a week, late at night after she had finished working and put her son to bed. The MGB agents, particularly the commanding officer Aleksandr, tried to convince her to divorce her husband because he was a spy. It was unpatriotic, they claimed, to be married to him. They told her she wouldn't be able to manage without him, her son needed to grow up with a father, and she should marry a Russian. Miriam refused to comply with their demands. She made it clear she would never divorce the father of her child. But the interrogations continued.

Jews suffered a terrible time in Russia between 1952 and 1954.

In railroad stations, travelers would spit on them. People denigrated the Jews while waiting in food lines. Billboards with caricatures of Jews accused them of being anti-Stalin. Miriam, confused by her nationalistic feelings that supported Stalin, and her belief that he had betrayed the Russian people, chose to not speak badly of Stalin. Like many others, she feared the consequences. To keep up appearances, she even escorted her kindergarten students to see the Tomb of the Unknown Soldier, which commemorated all the soldiers who had died for Stalin, including her brothers Simeon and Emile.

When Stalin fell ill and was being tended to by Jewish doctors the government recognized as the best physicians available, no one seemed to mind that the doctors were Jewish. But when he suffered a stroke and died shortly thereafter on March 6, 1953, rumors flew that the Jewish doctors treating Stalin had poisoned him. Many brainwashed Russians cried in the streets. They thought the world had ended because their idol no longer existed. Other Russians danced for joy! In the labor camps of the Gulag in Siberia, guards would shout at prisoners lined up for work early in the morning, "There are the Jews. They did experiments on Stalin and killed him. Death to all Jews."

The ensuing power struggle to become Stalin's successor took about six months. In September of 1953, in an emergency session of the Politboro, Nikita Khrushchev was given the title of First Secretary of the Communist Party's Central Committee. He didn't like Stalin and publicized Stalin's criminal record of killing millions of Russians and Poles and putting innocent people in jail. He accused Stalin of destroying Jews and non-Jews, even those from his hometown of Gori, Georgia. He reminded people of the numbers too large to count of Poles Stalin had imprisoned in Siberia. Miriam hoped Khrushchev's attitude would make life better for the Jews, but nothing much changed.

During her four months of questioning at the MGB social service meetings, Miriam often met alone with the commanding officer Aleksandr. She would tell him how she was struggling to raise her son alone. She would cry about her situation, the loss of her husband. Aleksandr would hold her in his arms to comfort her. An unusually sensitive man, he always calmed her. Sometimes, if he interrogated her alone, he would express his compassion for her and all the Jews who had been victims of crimes committed against them, or confide that he didn't think Aaron was guilty. He knew he was endangering himself by siding with a Jewish woman, but he felt compelled to help her.

Miriam appreciated Aleksandr's warmth and kindness, the way he held her. She softened under his touch. Still, Aaron was all she could think about. She had read the book he sent her, "Russian Wives before the Revolution," that depicted the dedication of prisoners' wives who had moved to Siberia to work and be near their husbands. Young and impressionable, Miriam believed she, too, should sacrifice herself and her life to live near Aaron. It wouldn't be easy raising money and finding help to travel there. And the weather might be too cold for her young son. No matter what befell them, though, they would be a family together again.

Although Miriam sent packages regularly to Aaron in the Gulag camp, she was becoming personally involved with Aleksandr. She sensed he felt more for her than she did for him, so she wasn't surprised at one of their meetings when he handed her a letter professing his love for her. After that, they did a lot of talking. Aleksandr suggested they start dating to get to know one another better. Miriam told him nothing could come of a relationship between them because she wouldn't betray Aaron, and she planned to take her son Martin to Siberia so the family could be together.

In his second letter, Aleksandr wrote that he would never stop loving Miriam or admiring her. He said that if she would accept him as a friend, he would be honored. Then he had to leave town on business for two and a half weeks. When he returned, he gave Miriam a lovely silver watch as a present. She knew she should give it back to him—she prided herself on being independent and didn't want to feel obligated—but she liked it so much she decided to keep it. Aleksandr was offended because she had intimated he was trying to "buy" time with her. He insisted he only meant to make her happy. In his next letter he told her farewell. Miriam was relieved, but she felt crushed at the same time.

A week later Aleksandr invited Miriam to meet him at a park in town. He handed her another letter and asked her to read it aloud. This time he had written her a poem expressing his undying love for her, asking her to pretend she loved him, even if only for a moment, saying they could change their destiny.

After she recited the poem, Miriam's heart melted. She hadn't expected to fall in love with Aleksandr, but she couldn't say "no" any more. They were discreet, often walking in the park while the rest of the town slept. Sometimes they'd sit on a park bench and talk. And always Aleksandr would give her letters and poems professing his love or his sadness. The beauty and truth of their love, especially after they had been intimate, belied the impossibility of their future together. For whenever Aleksandr tried to convince Miriam to divorce Aaron, she refused. Aleksandr may have been the man of her dreams, but Aaron was the father of her child and she would wait for him to be released.

Miriam had to work hard as a kindergarten teacher to make a living. Under the Soviet system, everyone suffered. A teacher earned the same salary as a street sweeper or a doctor. In order to supplement her income, with financial backing from Aleksandr and use of his government connections, Miriam hired a government driver to help her in a new business venture once a week on his day off.

At night, while Martin was in bed and the Russian couple watched over him, Miriam's driver would take her to a town half an hour away where she could buy good, prepared food, cheaply. Then he would drive her a few hours to Kiev to sell the food at a marked-up price to a few women she knew who ran a food stand. On the way back to Tarashcha she slept in the car. She arrived home by seven or eight in the morning, just in time to wake up Martin, prepare breakfast, and go to work.

The extra money she earned she sent to Aaron. He, in turn, would give some of this money to the prison doctor as a bribe so he wouldn't have to work outside in the bitter weather. He used the rest of the money to take courses to learn how to become a sewing machine technician. Soon Aaron achieved the status of "chief mechanic", which enabled him to teach his craft. This, combined with his ability to recite Talmudic prayers from memory during the holidays, gained him the respect of many prisoners. They looked up to him. Some even called him "Rabbi".

Miriam's son Martin was almost five years old when his father had been taken away by the MGB. He often asked about Aaron, where he was and why he didn't come home. Rather than tell him the truth, Miriam would lie and say he was working out of town, making money for the family. A smart young boy, Martin learned to be independent, and Miriam would let him go to the breadlines alone because they lived in a safe neighborhood. He knew people didn't think highly of Jews, and he told the other children at school he was not Jewish. He claimed that because he liked borscht, he was Ukrainian.

When Aleksandr shared rumors of a not yet officially announced plan to send Polish prisoners back to Poland in 1958, he explained that Khrushchev's earlier denouncements of Stalin's policies practically insured the exchange would take place. Aleksandr, who wished for Miriam's happiness whether it was with him or Aaron, advised her to go to the Polish embassy in Moscow. There she could find out which required documents she would have to file to leave Russia when the plan became official.

For her "vacation" from work in 1954 Miriam decided the time was right to take nearly eight year old Martin to Siberia to see his father and then travel to Moscow. She packed two large suitcases filled with eggs, pears, apples, salami and other food for Aaron to share with his friends. Wearing the only nice dress she owned that she had sewn for herself, with her son in tow, Miriam began the difficult five-day train ride to Siberia. The train was full of farmers, soldiers and other people reading newspapers. Martin didn't like sitting still and often jumped up and ran down the hall singing a Russian hymn. Miriam felt nervous. She could hear herself yell at Martin to be quiet and stay in his seat, but he paid her no heed. Then the soldiers told him to listen to his sister because she shouldn't have to yell at him. Miriam looked so young they didn't realize she was his mother.

When they finally arrived at the prison, Miriam tried to stifle her disdain for the cold, dreary tundra. She wasn't prepared for what she saw while she and Martin waited for Aaron in the waiting room. She cried at the sight of the soldiers using German Shepherds and automatic rifles to guard the prisoners as they marched them to work to cut trees. She imagined that at any moment she might see Aaron being mistreated. But instead, she and Martin were led to the classroom where he taught. For the next two days they talked about the past, how fortunate they were to be together, and the possibility of moving to Poland. Aaron approved of Miriam traveling to Moscow on the way home to inquire about how to proceed.

The trip to Moscow gave Miriam and Martin—both of whom were emotionally drained from their visit with Aaron—an opportunity to relax and sleep on the train. Once they arrived in the bustling capital, Miriam connected with a friend of Aleksandr's who drove them to the government center. Inside the building, Miriam met several women who also planned to go to Poland with their prisoner husbands. They shared information about what they needed to do when the prisoner transfer policy would become official.

Aaron was trained in sewing machine repair in Siberia

Vacation over, Miriam returned to Tarashcha, back to her life of struggle and love. Shortly thereafter, in 1955, she was fired from her teaching position. Word had gotten out that she was planning to move to Poland. Anyone voluntarily moving to Poland or Israel was labeled a "traitor". Consequently, the school didn't trust her with the children. But her friends at work gave her a nice going away party anyway, which made Miriam happy.

Pressure was mounting. No work. No money. Miriam created her own garden with tomatoes, potatoes, and a big pear tree, and she and her son harvested and ate their homegrown food. Because their crops yielded more than they needed, Miriam used her driver to take her to Kiev twice a week to sell the produce at a profit, which earned her enough to buy extra staples for her and Martin.

By 1956 Miriam knew she had to remove herself from the beautiful relationship she and Aleksandr shared. She didn't want to hurt him, because she loved him, but she couldn't stay with him. Sooner or later she would be reunited with Aaron. Aleksandr understood, although he was devastated. Shortly after they separated, he was sent to another headquarter site outside Tarashcha in Kiev. Or perhaps, Miriam thought, he had asked to be transferred. In February of 1957, she received two beautiful farewell poems from him, avowing his undying love for her.

Life wasn't easy without Aleksandr's love and financial and emotional support, but Miriam continued to work and raise her son as best she could. She didn't know what the future held. She didn't know how she would feel moving to Poland to be with her husband whom she hadn't lived with for so many years. Fortunately, she had two good single friends who visited her at night after work to cheer her up. During the summer, while Martin was away at a summer camp, they took her swimming in a lake and later to some pretty gardens. They told her it might be good for her to have a male friend, even if she wasn't going to divorce Aaron, because she deserved the help of a man. Why should she be made to suffer more?

It was at the lake, in 1957, that Miriam met Leonard. The moment they met, Miriam felt she knew him. She had seen him in town before, but had never made a connection with him. They spoke briefly until Miriam had to leave. Then one day when she was standing on the street outside her house, thinking about Leonard, he suddenly appeared. As they gazed into each other's eyes, the chemistry took over. It was just one of those things that happened, as if they had known each other forever. Many years later Leonard would write to

Miriam telling her that when he first saw her, before he even knew her name, he had already loved her and longed for her.

A playboy-type lawyer, Leonard seemed to come along in Miriam's worst time of need. She knew he had plenty of money because he was a director of a large company. He could help provide for her and Martin. And she liked him. With Aleksandr's backing gone, she had to find another way to support herself. Soon Leonard started sending a truck from his business that brought coal to her home on a regular basis so she and Martin could stay warm.

Leonard was very taken with Miriam—he claimed she was the only woman he had ever loved in this special way—and Miriam allowed herself to get involved with him. Out of all the women he had known, Miriam had stolen his heart. She didn't tell him about her unrequited love for Aleksandr, only about her vow to wait for Aaron. Leonard understood Miriam's situation and wished to honor her desire, but after a year he proposed to her. She, of course, refused. They continued to see one another a year-and-a-half longer and remained friendly after that.

While Miriam was waiting to go to Poland, a female friend of Aaron's who was a communist manager of a small service company hired Miriam to work in her office. Unfortunately, the woman's husband took a liking to Miriam and became sexually aggressive with her. She didn't dare tell his wife for fear of losing her job. And she managed to keep him at bay for a year by always crying loudly when he harassed her.

Hoping that the prisoner transfer policy she'd been hearing about for the last four years would soon become official, Miriam, on pure instinct, went to Moscow in 1958 to begin the paperwork necessary for her and her son to leave Russia. She feared she wouldn't be permitted to go because no one was being let out of Russia. And she felt helpless. If the government wouldn't allow Russian wives to travel to Poland to be with their husbands, she hoped she could move to another state, get a new job, and support her son and herself. She wrote to her mother's family in Crimea about her situation and received an invitation to come live with the family. She also wrote to her brother Aleksandr for advice, but he wouldn't tell her what to do. He knew he had already made her unhappy by insisting she marry Aaron. He didn't want anything else to go wrong.

Miriam needed money for whatever she was going to do, and she hoped someone in the family could help her. She decided not to ask her brother because he had barely enough to take care of his wife and children. Instead, she wrote to a cousin who ended up loaning her two hundred rubles which Miriam would repay when she sold her duplex. Things were looking up and Miriam felt good about getting ready for her Poland adventure. Even though it required a lot of preparation and determination … *courage,* too. Miriam dove into the project with enthusiasm. She wondered what kind of new life awaited her in Poland.

CHAPTER 10

Aaron's Release

When Polish President Gomulka and Russian President Brezhnev signed the pact to exchange prisoners, all Polish prisoners serving time in Russia were sent back to Poland. Aaron was given security papers and transported in a police van with Russian security across the southeastern border between Russia and Poland to the town of Przemyśl. There he spent three days in a Polish jail, where he was fed and treated kindly. Next, Polish security guards took him by train to his trial in Warsaw. Within three hours, the Polish government released him to a representative from the Israeli Embassy who arranged for his return to Przemyśl. The representative gave him money and the address of a Jewish synagogue in Przemyśl that would house him for a few weeks. Inspired with renewed hope, Aaron telephoned Miriam.

Miriam nearly burst into tears when she heard Aaron's voice on the phone. She couldn't believe he was free. She told him that as soon as she sold her half of the duplex, she and Martin would join him in Poland. He assured her they would live in a lovely home because the embassy and the Jewish community were helping him find suitable housing in Zabrze.

Moving to Poland was a major task for Miriam. She consulted with Leonard, now a good friend. He offered to help her sell her home and tend to whatever legal details were necessary for the trip.

Inasmuch as she wouldn't be permitted to bring any money into the country, he recommended Miriam buy products not available in Poland to sell there after she arrived. She bought a washing machine and a television and a motorcycle, which Leonard later shipped to her. Within six months, in the winter of 1959, Miriam and her son left for Poland. Martin had been almost five years old when his father was taken away. Now he was almost twelve.

CHAPTER 11

A New Life in Poland

When Miriam and Martin arrived in Zabrze in 1959, Aaron met them at the train station. The family reunion brought them all to tears. Together they were sad, nervous and excited, all at the same time. Although Miriam had dreamed of the day she would be with her husband again, the reality of seeing him face to face struck a strange note in her heart. She hadn't expected him to be free for another thirteen years. For Aaron, who had spent every day of his imprisonment imagining his freedom, nothing meant more than this moment with his family. It seemed unbelievable to both of them that they were really together.

The coal mining town of Zabrze had been invaded by Germans during the war. Their luxurious residences were left abandoned after they were forced to return to Germany. Prisoners like Aaron, most of whom had been imprisoned under false circumstances, were now being offered opportunities to enjoy these beautifully furnished apartments. Miriam loved their new home.

Soon the family settled down to everyday life. Aaron, a supervisor of sewing machine technicians, would leave early in the morning and travel half an hour by train to work in a factory in Katowice. He'd go to work every day wearing a clean white shirt and come home with his shirt black from the coal soot in the factory. Miriam didn't particularly like the soot being brought into the apartment, but she appreciated Aaron working to support them. She busied herself by unpacking and keeping Martin occupied. Soon she enrolled him in a Jewish/Polish school. Everyone seemed happy. But Miriam's life was again changing dramatically.

Aaron had spent many years without her and had become somewhat sexually demanding. Miriam, accustomed to the more romantic relationships she shared with Aleksandr and Leonard, felt uncomfortable being forced to have intimate relations. Suddenly the apartment seemed very dark to her, like the dirty coal-mining town itself.

Miriam was bored. She dreamed of another life, another time. She missed her brother, who was living in Kiev, and she realized she missed Russia. Her former lovers, Aleksandr and Leonard, still occupied her mind. So, hoping she might run into Aleksandr in Kiev, she made plans to visit her brother under the pretense of buying nylons—which couldn't be found in Poland—to bring home and sell.

Visiting with her brother and family and seeing cousins brought Miriam great joy. She reflected on her relationship with Aaron and wondered why, since she loved him, she wasn't genuinely happy with him. Always the romantic, she hoped she could locate Aleksandr. She missed his poems, his tender touch, his adoration. She even fantasized about leaving Aaron and starting over again with her former lover. But her fantasy dream turned into a nightmare when she saw him walking down the street, arm in arm with a stunning woman. Oh how her heart ached.

Later that night, alone in bed, Miriam examined the reality of her situation. She decided to focus on making her marriage work and not be involved in an outside romantic relationship. She wanted to move her family to a cleaner, healthier environment. She knew that hardships could lie ahead and she didn't want to be distracted from her mission. Instead of buying nylons to sell, she managed to get a good deal on a chinchilla coat, which would bring in a lot more money. When Miriam returned home to Poland, Aaron sold it to an old man who bought the coat for the young Jewish beauty at his side. Miriam's heart may have been broken in Kiev, but the suit-case full of money she received for the sale helped her heal. Well, not much.

Miriam in Poland, 1959

Miriam heard from friends that many Polish Jews were moving to Israel because Poland's antisemitism wasn't declining. If she had had a choice of where to relocate, she would have choosen the Unit-ed States. The land of the American Dream people spoke about in-trigued her. But Aaron had dreamed of going to Israel, the Promised Land, from the time he was a young boy. Israel, the homeland. He believed that if the persecuted Jews would have had their own coun-try sooner, the Holocaust might not have happened. Even the Span-ish Inquisition of the 1600s might not have occurred if the Jews had had a land to migrate to. Because of her loyalty to Aaron, Miriam agreed to relocate to Israel.

In their conversations about moving to Israel, Miriam suggested they also consider applying for permission to emigrate to Australia and the United States so they would have a backup plan if their ap-plication to Israel was denied. She reasoned that inasmuch as she and Aaron would use their Russian passports to apply for American im-migration—Russian citizens weren't permitted to leave Russia, which meant few were trying to enter the country—they stood a good chance of being approved much sooner than the usual six to seven years Poles had to wait. Maybe they'd be granted entry to America before Israel or Australia approved them. That was her hope.

For about a year, Miriam had been communicating with her old friend Clara Tututunik who lived in Szczecin, an industrial center and important Polish seaport. She had asked Clara to keep her ears open for any apartments for sale or rent on the water.

When Clara wrote back that she knew a German woman who was selling a lovely apartment, Miriam took the next train and traveled four-and-a-half hours to see it. She liked the spacious two-bedroom apartment. She loved the fresh sea air. And she offered, in trade, the motorcycle she had bought in Russia. Deal accepted, Miriam returned home and began packing. Aaron didn't like the idea of moving without a job, but she assured him he wouldn't have any trouble finding work.

Miriam adored Szczecin, a vibrant city filled with light and clean air and sea smells. She felt at home because many Russian immigrants lived there. Aaron liked it too. He found a higher paying supervisory position in a factory and Martin attended a Jewish private school financed by ORT, an organization that helped Jewish refugees.

Miriam spent most of her time with Clara, who turned out to be a good friend. She took Miriam to a social club and introduced her to her friend Vera, the most beautiful woman Miriam had ever seen, and her husband Victor. Soon, a close friendship developed between Miriam and Vera. They both were married and their husbands wanted to move their families to Israel. Miriam knew that firms in Israel were offering accounting jobs, so she and Vera signed up for courses at an accounting school run by the local university.

Although Miriam kept busy as a mother, wife and student, she still occasionally dreamed of being a movie star. She imagined she was already too old, but ... If she could work in Israel, she reasoned,

she could make enough money to study acting and perhaps
start out in a local production.
With this goal in mind, Miriam
devoted herself to the successful completion of her accounting studies. She tried not to
think about her former lovers
in Russia, and she pretty much
ignored the Polish men who
flirted with her.

Aaron waited patiently to
receive word about their travel
requests. He preferred to move
to Israel rather than the United States, but he also wanted to
find his Uncle Max who lived

Miriam and Aaron in Poland, 1961

in Miami Beach, Florida in America. He wrote notices in the Jewish
newspaper, *THE JEWISH DAILY FORWARD*, with hopes of connecting with him. No one responded.

Nearly a year later, a friend who had lived in a shtetl with Aaron's
uncle sent a letter from California saying he had contacted Aaron's
uncle. Next came a letter from Uncle Max. He offered to do anything
he could to bring Aaron and his family to the States. When Aaron informed him they were planning to move to Israel, his uncle insisted
they come to Miami Beach instead. He owned the San Juan Hotel on
the ocean where they could stay and look for work. Once they came
to America, he wrote Aaron, they would be with family. Then they
could travel to Israel or Australia any time they wished.

Meanwhile, Clara's application to travel to the United States had
been accepted. Before she left for Philadelphia, she encouraged Mir-

iam and her family to move there too, but Miriam felt bound to her husband and his wishes to go to Israel. Soon, though, Miriam and Aaron learned that many of the people who had moved to Israel were struggling. They had both suffered so much from the war years that neither of them felt like leaving their good life to suffer more.

It seemed fortuitous that Aaron's uncle had signed an affidavit to pay for their airline tickets to America, and they accepted his invitation. Clara, who worked in a catering business, was delighted Miriam would be coming to the States. She sent letters giving Miriam advice on how to prepare for the trip.

A month or two after Miriam finished accounting school in 1961—she graduated in two years with top honors—the Gopmans received their travel documents. They went to the American Embassy in Warsaw for medical tests to ensure they were healthy. They also had to undergo mental examinations. Then they were told to go back to Szczecin and wait for their tickets.

Miriam began preparations for the trip, and soon the airline tickets arrived from the embassy. Inasmuch as regulations prevented the Shirs from taking the same items to the United States they had been planning to take to Israel, Miriam remembered Clara's advice and sold their washing machine and television. She placed their shoes and clothing in a consignment shop. She had to pack the rest of their valuables—Aaron's German Veritas, the top of the line home electric sewing machine with a wooden stand they had brought from Zabrze, all her crystal, silver, three sets of dishes (each a service for twelve), beautiful bedding, feather pillows, comforters, and other belongings—in a cargo container that would be shipped on the train. The Gopmans would be allowed to bring the equivalent of only ten American dollars each in cash.

Miriam couldn't wait to go to America. It seemed like a dream come true. She loved living in the seaside port, but now she might have the opportunity to study acting in the United States. Because she imagined that Aaron's uncle was rich—he had to be if he could afford to buy three plane tickets for them—Miriam looked forward to enjoying the lavish American lifestyle she had heard about for so many years in Russia. Fourteen-year old Martin, however, didn't want to live in a capitalistic society. He had been raised in social-ist countries, which made Israel more appealing to him. But Aaron and Miriam convinced him what a wonderful life they could lead in America. Aaron explained that although moving to Israel had been his lifelong dream, he wanted the Gopmans to live near family.

In order to impress Aaron's uncle, Miriam bought new clothes for her family to wear on their journey to America. She dressed Aaron in a beautiful coat, Martin in a suit and tie. She wore fur gloves and a fur coat. On the winter day in 1962 that they were leaving Poland, many of their friends gathered at the train station to say goodbye to the Gopmans. Although Vera and Victor still planned to go to Israel, they boarded the train and traveled with their friends to the Amer-ican Embassy in Warsaw. After a sad and teary farewell, The Gop-mans continued on to the airport and boarded the Russian-made plane that would fly them to London. Miriam could feel the golden shores of America beckoning.

The rocky flight on the small propeller plane to London made Miriam so sick that she vomited several times during the trip. When they arrived in London to board their connecting flight, she breathed a sigh of relief at the sight of the Pan American World Airways plane. The smooth flight in the American jet proved to be a delightful im-provement. Martin and Aaron slept most of the way. Miriam stayed awake envisioning the new life she would soon be living. She felt truly blessed.

CHAPTER 12

Freedom in America

*I*mpeccably stylish in their finest apparel, Miriam and her family could easily have won first prize for the best-dressed refugees in New York when they deplaned at Idylwild Airport in the winter of 1962. Aaron's Uncle Max, aka Morris Gopman, met them at the gate with hugs for everyone. He told them in Russian that he was taking them to New York City to stay at a friend's hotel. During the taxi ride he explained how he had come from Kremenets in Ukraine. The pre-Revolution pogroms had driven his family out of Russia in 1917. His memory of a Russia with no cars and no electricity differed from Miriam and Aaron's. They had owned a radio and, after the war, a windup hi-fi set and color television. Getting used to the modern life in America had been difficult for Max. He didn't believe in capitalism when he came to America, but he had grown to enjoy its benefits. He tried to impress those virtues upon young Martin by explaining his ideas about American finance.

In the city, they walked on crowded sidewalks flanked by tall buildings and more restaurants than Miriam had seen in her lifetime. As they passed what appeared to be elegant, expensive hotels, Miriam wondered which one they'd be staying in. She was not happy when they arrived at a somewhat run-down building sandwiched between two swanky residences and Uncle Max ushered them inside. She had come to America. She wanted to stay somewhere at least as nice as their apartment in Szczecin!

When it came time to eat, Uncle Max picked a well-known side-walk cafe for the family to sample typical American food: hamburgers and hot dogs, French fries, malted milk shakes. Sitting at an outside table, they watched the parade of Americans passing by. Then they walked to Macy's, the great American department store. Miriam was impressed that shoppers didn't have to wait in line to buy shoes or dresses like they did in Russia. Plus, the American toys resembled none she had ever seen in Russia. Martin was fascinated by them, and Uncle Max bought him several.

Next on their list of things to do was a visit to Liberty Island. On the ferry ride there, Max explained some of the history of the Statue of Liberty and nearby Ellis Island, the now defunct federal immigration station closed in 1954. They marveled at the presence of the iconic statue—a symbol of freedom, new opportunities, and the American Dream—the national ethos of America. During the tour, Uncle Max translated the famous inscription that welcomed immigrants to the shores of the United States. Later in the day, he brought them to a meeting of an organization of people who had moved to the States from his hometown in Russia. Everyone was warm and friendly in welcoming the Gopmans to America.

On the second day of their stay in New York, the Gopmans strolled along Fifth Avenue. Miriam enjoyed window shopping. She couldn't believe the abundance of items available for purchase. What puzzled her, though, was that Americans didn't seem to care about the way they dressed. They wore sneakers and jeans. In Russia, everyone was decked out to the nines on the streets. Yet here in the country where Americans had so much of everything, nobody bothered to make a fashion statement. Miriam liked New York, the grandness of it all, but she was eager to fly to Miami in the morning.

When the exquisitely-dressed Gopmans and Aaron's uncle arrived at the airport in Miami, they were greeted by their Miami family. Miriam was shocked to see Uncle Max's two sons and their children—one of whom was Martin's age and two younger—wearing shorts and dirty tee shirts. She was more surprised that Aaron's Aunt Helen, who had been busy preparing dinner, had forgotten to remove her apron. America was a very different place indeed!

Uncle Max drove them all to his apartment in Miami Beach. As Miriam walked inside, she did a double take. She couldn't understand why Aaron's "rich" uncle who had spent most of his life in America lived in a one-bedroom apartment with very small windows facing the garbage outside. She had expected much more. Uncle Max realized Miriam's displeasure from her frown and quickly explained his situation. Years before he had moved from New York to Miami Beach because he needed the warm weather for his health. He had actually slept on a bench for months saving money to buy or lease a hotel. Now he owned two hotels, but he only owned a few shares with some partners. Mortgaged to the hilt, he was cash poor. In fact, he confided, he owed so much money on the mortgage for the hotel that his wife had to assist him with the cleaning so he wouldn't have to pay someone else to do the work. He hoped the Gopmans would pitch in and help.

Miriam didn't like hearing about Max's financial problems. She worried how they would all manage. She tried to focus on the fact that, regardless of his financial indebtedness, he had raised the money for Aaron and his family to leave Poland. She felt a debt of gratitude to him. How could she be angry at him? Admiring the beautifully set dinner table in the dining room, she blinked away tears when she noticed a rather large roasted turkey, considered a delicacy in Europe, with all the trimmings on a silver platter. Miriam could feel the love and warmth of Uncle Max, Aunt Helen and her friend who helped prepare the meal. Family and love. That was all that mattered. Everything would be okay.

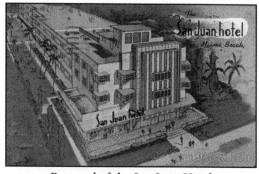

Postcard of the San Juan Hotel

After dinner, Aaron's uncle took them to the San Juan Hotel he owned on nearby Collins Avenue at Seventeenth Street. It looked like a nice place, right across from the ocean. Miriam felt nostalgic watching the older Russian Jews socialize in the hotel lobby. She wouldn't mind staying here, she thought. But being the height of the winter hotel season, no rooms were available except for a single basement room often used by the maintenance man. When Uncle Max showed them into their new home, Miriam tried to hide her disappointment at the small room with a double bed, a cot for Martin, a small refrigerator, shower and no TV. But she didn't hide it well. Uncle Max assured her that the tourists staying at the hotel for the winter would be going back north soon. Then Miriam could choose a larger, better appointed room for them to live in.

That first night Miriam was miserable. She wondered how long they would have to sleep in this tiny room. She had come to America to appease Aaron's family, but both she and Aaron also wanted to live the American Dream. In Russia, people believed that everyone in America was a millionaire. Well, this was not the America Miriam had dreamed about. Martin and Aaron felt terrible she was so unhappy. No matter how they tried to please her, they could do nothing to change her mood.

The next day Aaron's uncle handed Aaron a hundred dollars to start their new life. He also gave him two tickets to the Jewish theatre. In the early evening, he drove the whole family to a Chinese restaurant on Washington Avenue. Miriam and her family had never eaten Chinese food in Russia. Miriam savored the ribs so much, she swore she would never forget the delicious taste.

After dinner, they all walked along Lincoln Road, enchanted with the balmy weather, entranced by their new adventure. Then Uncle Max took the rest of the family home, and Miriam and Aaron set out for the Jewish theatre. But as luck would have it, while Aaron and Miriam were waiting in line, a pickpocket stole their tickets and the hundred dollars along with the thirty dollars Aaron had brought from Poland. What kind of a place was this America, they wondered, this land of dreams?

Miriam and Aaron didn't want to tell Aaron's uncle of their misfortune. They knew he was in no position to replace what had been stolen. But they had to tell him because they had no money. Uncle Max made them promise to not tell his wife what had transpired. He told them not to worry, that somehow he would find a way to give them more money. Miriam had just spent two days in Miami, and her idea of the American Dream was beginning to take on a frightfully different meaning.

The next morning, as Miriam got out of bed, she stepped into two inches of water. With each step toward the bathroom, she heard the carpet squish under her feet. Quickly she threw on some clothes and ran upstairs to the lobby. Uncle Max was positioned in the middle of guests trying to maneuver through the flood there. He signaled Miriam to come to him and instructed her to help calm the people. Poor Uncle Max had his hands full. But Miriam knew how to make people happy, so she began singing an old Russian tune. Some of the guests chimed in, and eventually everyone started laughing.

Life during the first two weeks in America held little promise. Miriam and Aaron couldn't speak English. They were broke and didn't know what to do to earn money. After enrolling Martin in public school, Aaron looked for work in a factory. In the meantime, Uncle Max introduced the family to the Russian immigrants from old Russia who had come to live in the hotel after the Revolution in the 1920s. It was easy to make friends with them because many spoke Yiddish or Hebrew, which Aaron did too. Miriam could say only a few words in Yiddish, but she picked it up quickly.

The old Russian Jews liked the Gopmans. The men gravitated to Aaron to discuss the Torah and religious matters. Several of the women hired Miriam to do alterations. She would bring her sewing basket and pincushion to their rooms, pin up their dresses or skirts to sew at home by hand. How exciting it was to earn two dollars a hem! That seemed like a lot of money. She altered sleeves too. But Aaron had to redo most of her sewing because she wasn't very good at it.

The Russians adored Martin. He ran errands and helped them at the pool, supplying towels or anything they needed. He didn't like the idea of accepting the monetary tips they offered him, but Uncle Max explained he should accept them because tipping was part of the American way. Soon Martin had saved enough money to go to Royal Castle every day after school and buy a hamburger and soup for a dollar. He was proud of himself. Maybe capitalism wasn't so bad after all, he thought.

Although Miriam didn't like living in the basement, she remained cheerful. It wasn't uncommon for the room to flood, leaving the floor covered with seawater and sand. She didn't mind because she didn't spend much time there, and the floor had mostly dried up by the time evening came. She liked working in the hotel office several days a week while Martin attended school. She answered the switchboard and used her accounting skills to help Uncle Max. In addition to the fifteen dollars a week he paid her, before she knew it, the Russian women raised her pay to five dollars a hem. It felt good to be independent again.

Now she desired to learn English. And she knew just the place to do it. Not far from the San Juan, the local movie theatre played American films all day. She spent part of her earnings and all her days off watching and listening to movies in English. They thrilled her and saddened her. There, on the screen, famous actresses like Bette Davis and Audrey Hepburn were living the dream she had imagined for herself. Miriam reveled in their artistry, but she was beginning to accept that she was meant to pursue a different career.

Aaron searched tirelessly for work until he landed a job with the Singer Sewing Machine Company in Coral Gables. Five days a week he rode the bus to his small office. He usually ate a sandwich brought from home at his desk while the other workers went out to lunch.

Once, on their way to lunch, his boss and a few employees told him to watch the door while they were gone. Aaron thought they said "wash" the door, so he took the door off its hinges and cleaned it thoroughly. When his coworkers returned, they laughed at what he had done. Embarrassed and ashamed, Aaron couldn't wait for the day to end.

On the way home he stopped in at his favorite bakery on Washington Avenue to pick up day-old bread and cake sold by the young Israeli woman who owned the shop. He always brought some kind of pastry for Miriam and Martin. Later that evening at dinner he told the family about his dreadful day. Everyone laughed, including Aaron. The following day he came home from work with good news. His boss had given him a five-dollar raise for taking the initiative to scrub the door. Aaron had been redeemed. Now he would be earning forty-five dollars a week.

Miriam acclimated well to this new life she hadn't anticipated. Seeing Uncle Max every day and socializing with the old Russian Jews gave her a sense of stability. Sometimes Aunt Helen would bring over homemade flanken, which Miriam would put in the refrigerator. Usually the Gopmans ate in their basement room. Occasionally they would enjoy a night out with Aaron's uncle's family and eat at the Famous Restaurant, which served Chinese and Jewish food. But for the most part, the families stayed to themselves.

After a month had passed, Uncle Max contacted a friend who hired Miriam to do alterations in his boutique. Miriam did the best she could, but she had to sew at the store, which meant Aaron couldn't help her. When a few customers complained, the owner appeased them. But one client screamed at her when she saw how Miriam had damaged her dress. A week later, Miriam was fired.

Next she worked in a sweatshop-style factory on N.W. Fifth Avenue in North Miami, an industrial avenue of stores and manufacturers, using an electric sewing machine to make collars in an assembly line. Her first day on the job, unbeknownst to Miriam, the bus system went on strike in the middle of the day. After work, she waited on the bus bench with several African Americans. One by one they soon walked away and she was alone. Nobody driving by stopped or paid attention to her. As the sun disappeared beyond the horizon, Miriam sat crying in the dark. Aaron came home from work and fell apart when he learned Miriam hadn't returned since she left in the morning. Martin told him that if the buses weren't running, his mommy was probably sitting on the bus bench, crying. Aaron immediately enlisted one of the Russian men to drive them to the bus stop. Sure enough, not far from the factory, he found Miriam sitting on a bench, crying, and he helped her into the car.

Miriam didn't know how to use the factory's electric sewing machine well, so she would sneak the collars out and bring them home to Aaron. He would stay up all night sewing for her. In the morning, she would sneak the finished collars back into work. This dishonesty created a great deal of stress for Miriam because she knew she'd be fired if she got caught. Sometimes she thought she'd throw up if she had to look at one more collar. But they were better than the yellow stars she had to sew in the ghetto.

Miriam didn't like to draw attention to herself at work for fear her lack of skill would be discovered. Once, when the owner/inspector Sylvia Greenwald was walking toward her, Miriam decided she could impress her by looking busy at her sewing machine. But she pressed down on the machine's pedal too hard and it whirred out of control. Miriam cried.

Sylvia stroked her shoulder and said, "Don't rush." But Miriam— whose comprehension of English was worse than her practically non-existent ability to speak it—thought she said, "You're not in Russia." Luckily, Sylvia's husband Morris spoke Russian and solved the confusion.

While Aaron was enjoying their life in the States, Miriam couldn't tolerate it. She regretted having come to America and resented having to work in a factory. She realized how lucky she was to never have had to work in a factory sweatshop in Russia.

She fantasized about leaving for Poland and flying to Israel where she could meet up with her friend Vera. With this thought in mind, she sought assistance from the Jewish Federation. The representative with whom she met informed her that Aaron's uncle would have to approve her travel plans because he had signed the original affidavit to sponsor her immigration. That information put an end to Miriam's fantasy.

Martin, meanwhile, was having his own problems adjusting. Enrolled in junior high school at the same grade level he would have been assigned in Russia, he was bored with schoolwork because he had received a higher level of education than his American peers. He didn't speak English well, but he excelled in math. He could solve problems his teachers couldn't solve, and they respected him. Often, though, he would come home crying, complaining about how the other students teased him. The only way he knew to fight back was to actually fight them and beat them up. That made the students admire his bravery, and no one ever bothered him again.

The Greenwalds, owners of the factory Miriam worked in, had no children of their own. Both in their seventies, they treated Miriam like a daughter. After Miriam had been at her job for just a few weeks, they invited her and Aaron to their home for lunch on the weekend. Miriam had never eaten vegetables with dip in Russia, and she imagined the dish was the main meal rather than an appetizer. Then the maid appeared and led them into another room where tuna fish was served. Miriam was enthralled by the formality of it all.

As time went by, the two couples enjoyed one another's company on a regular basis. Morris Greenwald taught Aaron how to fix American sewing machines, which enabled him to freelance as a mechanic for manufacturing factories. He then referred Aaron to several of his colleagues. Most of the manufacturers spoke Yiddish, and they appreciated Aaron's ability to communicate with them in their own language. The more money Aaron brought home, the more he wanted to work.

Soon the Greenwalds promoted Miriam to take over Sylvia's job as inspector in order to lighten Sylvia's work load. Miriam was thrilled she wouldn't have to sew any more. Thanks to their exclusive contract to manufacture Lilly Pullitzer's popular bright, colorful, sleeveless shifts, the Greenwalds' business was booming. Lilly's reputation as an eccentric socialite and fashion designer in her late fifties—usually clad in one of her floral print cotton shifts with rubber thongs and known to fly her own plane between Key West, Miami and Palm Beach—helped promote her line of clothing.

Miriam felt good about the relationship that developed with the Greenwalds. They were like family. When they told her they hoped she would take over the factory if they retired, she developed a new attitude about her work. She enjoyed trying to converse with the vivacious Latina sewing machine operators, and she taught them Russian. Now she sat on a high stool in the middle of the main floor at a big wooden table Morris had built for her. She checked every piece of clothing to make sure the seams were sewn straight. They often weren't.

Earning thirty-five dollars a week helped Miriam buy shoes for three dollars that she sent to her brother's family and cousins in Russia. She also saved money toward an apartment. But America was still not the heaven Miriam had expected it to be. She hated working in the factory with no air conditioning. It exhausted her. More accustomed to the cold temperatures of Russia and Poland, she detested the tropical heat. Their apartment didn't have air-conditioning either. Miriam practically lived in the cool movie theatre on days when she wasn't working and at night. That's where she became enamored of her heartthrob, Paul Newman. Her constant exposure to the films she loved helped her learn English quickly and fed her passion.

Three months after Miriam started working for the Greenwalds, she and Aaron had saved enough money to pay the two months security deposit and one month's rent—one hundred fifty dollars—to move into an apartment on Ninth Street and Pennsylvania Avenue in Miami Beach. The second floor apartment with two bedrooms divided by a kitchen and living/dining area seemed enormous compared to their hotel room. And what a luxury to have the bathroom in the master bedroom!

Within a week after moving in, the Gopmans paid to take their container from Russia out of storage. Miriam had forgotten about many of the items she had packed, and it delighted her to see them again. Now that she could use her china, she invited the whole family for Sunday lunch. She hadn't entertained in a long time, and as she shook out the beautiful beige linen tablecloth and watched it sail onto the table, she flashed back to times in Russia when her mother would prepare sumptuous dinners at holiday time. Setting the table with her finest china and crystal and silver pleased Miriam.

When everyone arrived, they praised Miriam for the festive spread she had laid out. They'd not seen plates and glasses of such quality and were surprised to learn they had been made in Poland. After they feasted on lox, bagels with cream cheese, herring with cooked potatoes, potato salad and a myriad of other Jewish foods, Miriam gave everyone a crystal glass, a vase, or a dish she had earmarked for each of them.

Luckily, when Miriam got pregnant again in 1963 and started experiencing morning sickness at work, the adoring Greenwalds moved out of their air-conditioned office and moved Miriam into it. She could finally breathe better at work, but her apartment was sweltering. One day Aaron brought home a big fan on a stand he had found in the garbage at a nearby building. He and Martin would carry it from room to room, wherever Miriam set herself down, to keep her cool.

In May, by her ninth month, Miriam had become too uncomfortable to work. A friend of Aaron's uncle offered to let her stay in a fully stocked, huge cabana at a hotel he owned. Here Miriam relaxed in the comfort of the ocean breeze and the warm salt water. Two weeks later, on May 16, 1964, she was rushed to the hospital and delivered a beautiful baby girl, Rita.

The thought of returning to the hot apartment with her baby upset Miriam, but before she left the hospital she was informed that she could stay in the cabana again until she was ready to move back home. Blessed with a free place to care for Rita, Miriam received another blessing when the Greenwalds sent a woman to help her with the baby for two weeks. The woman refused to take any money from Miriam and told her she should help the next person she met in need. Every day the Greenwalds came to visit, bearing toys and clothes made by Miriam's coworkers.

Aaron, meanwhile, was busy negotiating to buy a car and a house. With the help of his uncle, who co-signed the note, he purchased a house in North Miami Beach for thirteen thousand dollars with no money down. When the Gopmans moved to their new home, Miriam felt better than ever. She had a wonderful husband, two beautiful children, and a home of her own with air conditioning in the living room and bedrooms. By now her Russian dream of movie stardom had faded, but she was living the American Dream, and it had only just begun.

Morris Greenwald continued to help Miriam however he could. Miriam, independent and ambitious, wanted to resume working so she could have her own income, but she couldn't leave Rita unattended. Morris came up with the idea of hiring Miriam to take care of his seventy-year-old sister in Miriam and Aaron's home during the daytime. She suffered from Parkinson's Disease, which made it challenging for Miriam to juggle the responsibilities of caring for her daughter and Morris's sister. But, as usual, she rose to the occasion.

Before long, Aaron and Miriam opened the Universal Sewing Machine Company in 1964 with the intention of selling industrial sewing machines. Their research indicated that Cubans were fleeing

Fidel Castro's government in droves. Cuban women working in factories during the day and sewing at home at night needed commercial sewing machines. Aaron placed ads in a local North Miami digest and Miriam acted as secretary taking messages while she tended to Morris's sister and Rita. After dinner Aaron reviewed the orders.

Martin helped too. A dean's list student who had received government loans to study engineering at the University of Florida, he would drive more than seven hours from Gainesville in the family's old blue and white Ford station wagon with his friends on the weekends to help his father assemble the sewing machines for delivery.

Word spread quickly throughout the Cuban community about the good sewing machines at reasonable prices. Within two to three years the business was turning a handsome profit.

CHAPTER 13

The Dusseldorf Trial

One evening in August of 1964, Aaron was reading THE JEWISH DAILY FORWARD (currently the FORWARD) when he noticed an ad placed by the German Embassy seeking information about any of the last three families known to be interned in Tarashcha, Ukraine during World War II. According to the ad, the Embassy believed a female named Maria Shir, most likely the sole Jewish survivor, might be living in Miami. She could be a very important witness to testify in Dusseldorf against the Nazi criminals who had invaded Tarashcha. A phone number was listed.

Aaron jumped up out of his chair and hurriedly told Miriam what he had just read. Surprised, terrified, excited, Miriam declared she would testify in Dusseldorf. Aaron said it would be too emotional for her, and he wouldn't let her go. She told him, in no uncertain terms, that she was going. Too many people believed the Holocaust never happened. She had to testify to keep the truth alive and validate the Holocaust. She had waited and waited for an opportunity to put those German monsters in jail, to make them pay for their crimes. Nothing could stop her now, not even her husband.

Miriam didn't sleep well that night with so many horrible memories stirring in her mind. She had never told anyone how, every night, she suffered from nightmares about the war. They terrified her, and she didn't want to talk about them. She hoped that testifying would bring everything out in the open and put an end to her sleepless nights.

The next day Miriam phoned the German Embassy. When she agreed to an examination as a witness of fact before an official from the Consulate General of the Federal German Republic, the friendly representative explained that another representative would contact her with more information about applications and interviews she would need to complete.

At her examination on December 28th, 1964 at the German Embassy in Miami, Florida, Miriam declared her preparedness to appear as a witness at the Landgericht (county court) in Dusseldorf and to testify against the Nazis and their slaughter of Russian Jews in Tarashcha in 1941.

In March of 1966 Miriam received a summons to appear in court in Dusseldorf as a witness on May 11, 1966 at 11 o'clock. Miriam was informed that representatives from various agencies would be contacting her to assist her to prepare for the trip, including a Russian translator from the University of Miami. In addition, the Embassy would arrange her travel to Dusseldorf—provide security, private doctors, psychiatrists, and nurses to be with her every day—and help her through the intense process of testifying. Also, a nurse would be sent to her home in the United States to take care of little Rita. The nurse would cook and clean to help Aaron and Martin too. Miriam would be given whatever she and her family needed to make the trip as easy as possible.

A difficult journey lay before her, but Miriam was finally going to be able to keep her promise to her mother and Mania that she would bring the Nazi criminals to justice. She would keep her promise to herself to do everything in her power to help the world ensure these atrocities never happened again. She believed it was her duty, her moral obligation to society.

Certified translation from the German language

DER LEITENDE OBERSTAATSANWALT
BEI DEM LANDGERICHT DÜSSELDORF   4.Düsseldorf.1., March 16,1966
                                     Mühlenstrasse 34

Reference Number : 8 I Ks 1/66
(Please quote in your reply)

Mrs.
MIRIAM G O P M A N
951 N.E. 172nd Street
M i a m i , Fla.
U.S.A.

Re: Criminal Proceedings against Karl J u n g and others
____because of aiding and abetting before the fact of murder.

Dear Mrs. Gopman :

Before the Court of Assizes at Düsseldorf on March 3 , 1966
the main hearing against six former members of the " Einsatzkommando 5 (special action detachment) has started. The
accuseds are being charged with taking part in the illegal
killing of Russian nationals - committed in the year 1941
in the Ukraine among other places at Taraschtscha.

At the occasion of your examination as a witness before one
of the officials of the Consulate General of the Federal German
Republic on December 28 , 1964 you have very kindly declared
your preparedness, when the occasion arises to personally appear
before the Landgericht at Düsseldorf as a witness. The President of the Court of Assizes has thereupon ordered that you
be summoned to kindly appear as a witness on May 11, 1966
at 11.00 hours. The official summons to this effect will
be sent to you shortly.

In case that you are prepared to accept the summons and you
should have the wish to not pay the costs of the journey to
Düsseldorf in advance yourself, I would be grateful to you
for your early reply,also to the effect whether you would
want to travel by plane or by ship. I would then immediately
take the necessary steps that in due time an air-travel ticket
respectively a ship's passage be handed over to you before
you start on the journey to Düsseldorf.

                          Yours sincerely

                               By order :

                          signed : (Grau)
                               Public Prosecutor
        -.-.-.-.-.-.-

It is hereby certified that the   *Karl Gottfried Werner*
above is a true translation of
the original document.
Düsseldorf, 19. Mar. 1966

The long flight to Frankfurt and then Dusseldorf allowed Miriam to reflect on her past and her present. She had grown up a happy child in a very wealthy family, endured horrors during the war, managed to stay alive in hiding, lived in Poland and learned accounting, emigrated to the United States and was living the American Dream. What more could anyone ask for? She knew the trial would take a toll on her, but feelings of excitement and happiness for all she had survived permeated her being.

On the runway at the airport in Dusseldorf, Miriam, wearing a tailored suit and carrying a small travel bag and leather purse, stepped off the plane and descended the portable stairway. Two men on the ground in suits and fedoras were waving to her. She swallowed hard, smiled down at them. The men introduced themselves, one as a representative from the German Embassy, the other a representative from the Israeli Embassy. They drove her to the hotel where she'd be staying. There she was guarded by two German police officers who stood watch outside her room. On the first morning of the trial, the guards escorted Miriam from her hotel to the trial courtroom along with the doctors and nurse who accompanied her. For the next two weeks they provided top security going to and from court.

When Miriam walked into the crowded courtroom, she noticed three long tables configured in a U shape with chairs around the outside of them and several men in black robes. Every table had a microphone. The judge, also wearing a black robe, was sitting alone at the head table placed horizontally in the front of the room. Seated to his left, at a table perpendicular to his, six Nazi war criminals in their 40s and 50s in prison uniforms were conversing with their middle-aged defense attorney. None of them looked familiar to her.

Miriam was guided to the table to the right of the judge, also perpendicular to his table, across from the criminals. Her attorney and

Prosecutor, the young translator, and a few official type people at her table introduced themselves and shook her hand. Quite a bit further from the judge, seated at two tables in an L shape, the stenographer, a representative from Yad Vashem (the official Israeli memorial of the Holocaust victims) and the press were busy taking notes. When Miriam turned around, she saw sitting behind her the doctors and nurse, two police officers and twenty people she later found out were family members of the soldiers on trial.

Shortly after the trial began, the Prosecutor addressed Miriam in German. The translator beside her translated the German words in her ear. When Miriam responded to questioning, the translator translated aloud in German simultaneously. In the beginning, the questioning centered on identifying the men on trial. But Miriam was only twelve when the Nazis had captured her. Thirty-five now, twenty-three years later, she didn't recognize them. She could, however, describe their actions in Tarashcha and answer questions about them. She would never forget what she had witnessed, especially not in her dreams.

Every day for two weeks, Miriam was forced to return to the time and place in her life that had changed her forever. She had to repeat detailed information about how she and the other children had been forced to sew the yellow Jewish stars on clothing, how and when the Nazis beat or whipped the children, how they beat the teachers, how they acted cruelly and degraded the Jews, and other deplorable actions they engaged in. Often her testimony was interrupted by tears. When she was describing the mass execution in Tarashcha's Babi Yar, saying she had thought the Nazis were going to kill them all, she screamed and exploded into hysterical sobbing. Her doctor had to sedate her. He told the judge her system was so flooded with adrenaline and hormones that she needed to rest. Court was adjourned until the next morning.

Miriam felt fulfilled that the whole world was finding out the truth about these Nazis. Even the German people as a whole were thankful the criminals were being exposed. But the trial devastated Miriam. Reliving the horror of her three-and-a-half years in the war made her physically ill. At first, she cried for three days straight. The doctors and nurses on call who stayed with her helped relieve her pain and distress. Each day, though, no matter how terrible she felt, she gave thanks that she had survived. She was going to incriminate the Nazi criminals, tell the world her true story, remind people of the cruelty and the evil of the Holocaust, impress upon humanity that it really did happen. She was living proof. She had survived to share the atrocities of the war and remind people to never let anyone inflict such destruction and devastation on any member of the human race as that suffered by the victims of Nazi cruelty.

By the end of her portion of the trial, five of the six Nazis had admitted to committing the atrocities Miriam had detailed as an eye witness of fact. She hadn't recognized the men by looks, but the final prisoner, Horst Guido Huhn, whose name rang a bell, turned out to be the colonel. He refused to accept responsibility for ordering the mass genocide in Tarashcha's Babi Yar or committing any other atrocities. He claimed he was just doing his job, following orders.

Exhausted from the grueling trial that was still ongoing after she had served as a witness, Miriam flew back to the United States and anxiously awaited the outcome. The Jewish Federation sent a representative to meet with her. The act of testifying had changed Miriam's life in a positive way, and she spoke freely to the representative about the trial.

Whereas most Jewish people did not want to talk about the Holocaust, Miriam felt more than ever it was her obligation to speak up and speak out, to deliver a message to the world about the importance of fighting for peace. She couldn't, however, bring herself to speak with her children about her own personal experience of the Holocaust.

In later years, if her daughter Rita questioned her, she would become emotionally upset. And if she had to watch a film about the Holocaust, she would get hysterical.

Although she returned to Russia in 1969 to visit her brother Aleksandr in Kiev—primarily to help prepare him and his family to come to the United States—Miriam never revisited Tarashcha. She had more than enough memories of the shtetl.

Good news arrived via a phone call not long after Miriam had returned from Germany. Thanks to her fortitude and determination, the colonel and two of the Nazi SS special squad leaders she had testified against were sentenced in Dusseldorf on August 5th, 1966 to prison terms for their part in the massacre of Jews in Tarashcha.

Tears streaming down her face, Miriam told Aaron the verdict was in and at least some of the Nazis would be incarcerated. Aaron put his arms around her. He congratulated Miriam for never giving up. He asked her how it felt to be validated and vindicated. She said that whenever she wished she could take back the past and be the little girl who wanted to be a movie star, she would laugh, because she had already played the best role of her life.

CHAPTER 14

Living the American Dream

Miriam soon became recognized and honored by the Jewish community for her historic role in proving the Nazi war criminals guilty. Many residents considered her a local hero. During the years after the trial, as a highly respected member of Temple Beth Torah and Hadassah, she volunteered for many activities. She also continued working with Aaron in their business. However, she wasn't particularly interested in sewing machines. Bored, Miriam wanted to do something she enjoyed.

In 1970, Miriam heard that a friend of Aaron's uncle was selling the Santa Barbara Hotel, a forty-room building on 20th Street, just off of prestigious Collins Avenue. The news piqued her interest. She knew the hotel business inside-out from her experience at the San Juan in her early years in America. She could prepare rooms, talk to the guests, use the switchboard, count the money. The idea suddenly sounded quite interesting, and Miriam realized she wanted her own business, her own income, her own responsibility to herself. It would be easy for her to run a hotel, she thought, just like she managed her home. Independent to the core, although she had no money for a down payment, she called and made an appointment to meet the owner.

Mr. Mandell welcomed Miriam into his office. He told her how much he had heard about her over the years, how he admired her courage and how she had changed the course of history by testifying against the Nazis. She asked him a lot of questions and wanted to look at the accounting books. After reviewing them and seeing what a sizeable profit she could earn, Miriam negotiated to buy the property. Mr. Mandell went out of his way to make the terms of sale acceptable to Miriam. Because he knew she had good credit, he told her she could give him a small down payment and pay him monthly. Now she just had to figure out how to come up with the down payment.

On her way home Miriam had a brainstorm. She could use the money she had been saving for Rita from cash gifted to her daughter for birthdays and replenish it with income from the hotel. That same day, without another thought, Miriam picked Rita up at school and drove to the bank to withdraw the money. She told her six-year-old daughter this money was going to make them rich.

Miriam's life became more complicated when she bought the Santa Barbara Hotel. Although she enjoyed meeting people and making their stay as pleasant as she could, she had to work very hard for the next nine years. By adding entertainment nights with famous stand-up comedians like Jackie Mason and Bob Newhart, she ensured the hotel would be full. To balance her work life, she became very active in Hadassah, and she and Aaron participated in temple activities and club meetings.

In 1974, Mr. Mandell contacted Miriam. He informed her that the owners of the Peter Miller Hotel had died. Their children had called on him because they needed money and didn't know how to sell the property. He encouraged Miriam to buy the hotel, a three-story building with eighty rooms, around the corner from the Santa Barbara on Collins Avenue and 20th Street. He felt certain she could acquire it at a good price, and he offered to negotiate the deal for her.

Peter Miller Hotel, 1973

Miriam enjoyed managing the two hotels, making sure the rooms were kept clean and that the guests were well taken care of. The Peter Miller had been a company hotel, mostly for executives. One day while she was in the basement sifting through the assortment of items strewn about, she came across a sign that said, "No dogs. No Jews." Recalling the torment of the Jewish people, of her own personal torment, Miriam sat down and sobbed. She wondered how human beings could treat other humans so cruelly, but she cried for only a few moments. All that was behind her.

Now the proud owner of two hotels, Miriam was earning good money and saving money too. She often had to work twenty hours a day during the fully-booked winter season, but she was happy with her success. Year after year the snowbirds would return, always eager to see Miriam. She had a good sense of humor, which endeared her to the guests. Her professional demeanor and eagerness to accommodate them helped her gain a reputation as an outstanding hotelier.

Meanwhile, by 1975, Miriam and Aaron's sewing machine business had become so successful they had to move to a larger factory. They found another building which they bought and remodeled. But they needed an experienced engineer to install their industrial machines. When they asked Martin to help, he took a year's leave of absence from his job as an engineer for Teledyne in Huntsville, Alabama. He traveled all over the world, especially to Japan, selling and installing the sewing machines. Definitely an asset to the business, Martin decided to stay on.

Every few years Miriam had saved enough money to put a down payment on another hotel or apartment building on the same block as her other hotels. Buying investment property was like playing Monopoly to her. At one point, in addition to her other holdings, Miriam owned two buildings next door to each other, which she connected through one switchboard. Over a period of years, she acquired a square block of buildings in the heart of Miami Beach and became known as the Queen of Miami Beach. As much as she enjoyed being a *grande dame* and hotelier, Miriam decided to sell her properties and retire in 1985.

When Aaron became ill in 1995, Miriam spent the next eight years taking care of him. In 2003 Miriam was voted Woman of the Year by the Oceania Chai Chapter of Greater Miami Region of Hadassah. While she was getting dressed to attend the meeting where she would receive her award, Aaron's nurse's aide came into the room and told her that Aaron was dead. Miriam wept for a while. Then she phoned Martin and Rita with the news.

For Miriam, the loss of her husband signaled the end of a lifetime of struggle ... and success. She and Aaron had achieved the American Dream. Now Miriam could enjoy the fruits of her labor. The Gopman family continued to thrive for many years. Rita graduated

Miriam and Aaron honored with the Lion of Judah Award, 1996

from Brandeis University and Harvard Law School. She is a highly respected partner in a law firm. Martin still owns and operates the company his parents began 53 years ago.

Miriam Gopman, the sole Jewish survivor of the Holocaust in Tarashcha, Ukraine, had come to the United States with only a few possessions and ten dollars in her purse. Her courage, quick mind, instinct, determination and charm, as both a child and a woman, helped her through difficult times and brought her good luck and fortune. Within fifteen years after her arrival in America, Miriam became a hero to many as the woman who testified against and helped incriminate Nazis at the Nazi War Crimes Trials in Dusseldorf, Germany. In addition, she helped bring prosperity to Miami Beach for many years. Not only was she acclaimed an extraordinary hotelier and given the title of The Queen of Miami Beach, she also raised funds for many Jewish organizations in her various roles in temple and Hadassah.

Today, Miriam resides in Sunny Isles Beach, Florida. She believes her life was spared so she could share her story and help ensure that the atrocities committed by the Nazis will never be repeated.

Miriam Shir Gopman

Born: MARIAM SHIR, March 18, 1929 (passport d.o.b. April 1) in Russia, near Kiev, shtetl of Tarashcha, Ukraine. She was the youngest of four children with three older brothers. All served in the military. Miriam's oldest brother Emile was also a blacksmith. He died in the war in Finland in 1940. The middle brother Simeon served in the Marines and was killed in April, 1945, when a ship struck a mine and all on board died. The youngest brother Alexander served in the Army. He died in the United States on May 3, 2001. Miriam married Aaron Gopman in 1946. They had two children, Martin and Rita.

Nickname: MUSIA. She used the name MARIA NESTERENKO when hiding as a Ukrainian orphan refugee.

Mother: RIVKA GREENFELD: She worked in the home.

Father: AARON SHIR: He owned his own blacksmith and carriage business with his father.

Husband: AARON GOPMAN was born December 17, 1919 in the shtetl of Vishnevets in Volan, Poland, near the Russian border (in 1939 it became part of Russia). The oldest of three children, he had two younger sisters. His father was in the business of buying products from farms and reselling them. His mother worked in the home. He died in the United States on March 30, 2003.

Son: MARTIN, born May 22, 1947
Daughter: RITA, born May 16, 1964
Grandchildren: Alexandra, Madeline and Hannah (Rita's children); Nathan (Martin's child)

Honors

Woman of Distinction: February 12, 2006, Hadassah acknowledges with special gratitude Miriam's sustained commitment and extraordinary dedication to Hadassah.

Woman of the Year: March 30, 2003, Oceania Chai Chapter of Greater Miami Region of Hadassah

Lion of Judah Award: 1996, for Miriam and Aaron in support of the Israel Bond Program

USC Shoah Foundation Institute for Visual History and Education (Stephen Spielberg, Founder): 1995, videotaped interviews of Miriam and Aaron as part of a collection and archive of testimonials from Holocaust survivors all over the world

The New Life Award: 1989, for Miriam and Aaron's "dedicated efforts and support to build a new life for the Jewish people and the State of Israel"

Honored with Aaron by the Ben Gurion Jewish Survivors' Club: 1987, for their annual commitment to the organization

Honored with Aaron by the Century Club of Beth Torah Congregation: 1985, for their annual commitment to the organization

Memberships

More than forty years as active member of Hadassah: Organized, developed and implemented Sunny Isles Chai Chapter in 1990.

    PRESIDENT 2003 & 2004, 1996, 1997 & 1998

    VICE PRESIDENT 1991-1996 and 2002 - present

    ("Present" indicates the time of this writing.)

2005 - present: member of Child Survivors of the Holocaust, South Florida Group, (children in hiding)

2001 – present: member of Temple Sinai

1997 – present: member of Concerned Citizens of the City of Sunny Isles

1964 – 1989: North Miami Beach Chapter of Hadassah

    Served as TREASURER in the 1980s

1989 – present: member of Habonim, Holocaust Survivor Culture Club

1980s – present: member of Ben Gurion Jewish Survivors' Club; Aaron served on the Board of Directors and was honored yearly for his active dedication and involvement.

1970s – present: active in IDF (Israeli Defense Forces), served as volunteer to raise funds for Friends for Israeli Defense Force

1964 – present: member of Beth Torah Congregation

Fern Ellis

*F*ern Ellis started penning thoughts and stories at the age of seven when her mother gifted her a heart-shaped diary. She earned a Master's Degree from Pepperdine University. Some of her career credits as a freelance writer include copywriting and scriptwriting for advertising agencies in Miami, Florida, and Los Angeles, California; interviewing and writing articles about renowned musicians for Ovation and The Fugue, former classical music magazines; developing and writing educational material for the Los Angeles Times; creating handbooks, teacher-training video scripts, and informational scripts to the California legislature for the Los Angeles Unified School District (LAUSD); co-authoring an early English as a Second Language textbook for Simon and Schuster; writing music and lyrics for songs she has recorded; writing publicity for Miami-Dade County Public Schools. She developed and implemented the first educational program for the homeless for LAUSD. Her twenty-year teaching career included classes in creative writing and composition, public relations, French, Spanish, English, ESL and the first women's history course at Miami Dade Community College, "History of Women in Modern America from 1857." Her manuscript, "Miriam Gopman: The Courage of a Hero and Her Story of Survival," appears in the national archives of the United States Holocaust Memorial Museum.

Made in the USA
Columbia, SC
11 December 2017